# Chakras

The true story of a medium

Halu Gamashi

# Chakras

The true story of a medium

2017

Ventos Antigos

www.VentosAntigos.com

G186c
   Gamashi, Halu, 1963-
   Chakras: The true story of a medium
   Halu Gamashi
   1st edition - Ventos Antigos, 2017
   1. Spirituality 2. Mediumship 3. Chakras
I. Gamashi, Halu II. Title
UDC: 133.7

**Cover**
Luciana Morin

**English Version**
Will James Masters and Silvia Nogueira

# Contents

# The start of the journey

I was part way through my journey when I started to write this book; somewhere between courage and fear.

I found myself somewhere between the Brazilian states of Bahia and São Paulo. When I'm in Bahia, I stay in Cacha Pregos, a little fishing village on Itaparica Island. I always return here to write my books, recharge my batteries and hide away from the rest of the world. In São Paulo, I live and work in a country house, close to the Castelo Branco Highway.

Ten years ago, when I wrote *An Apprentice's Journey,* I was at the start of my journey, innocently taking my first steps out into the unknown. Was I afraid? A little... but... it was a fear filled with wonder and expectation.

*An Apprentice's Journey* was my first book about the spiritual world, and was published by two publishing houses: Eureka and Rosa dos Tempos, the latter being the name of a branch of Grupo Editorial Record. In the book, I recount part of my experience with the spiritual world.

Back then I didn't have the opportunity to tell my whole story and, to be completely honest, I don't know if I ever will. So much has happened; only time will tell.

In this book, *Chakras: the true story of a medium,* I plough ahead, using the courage I've gained from overcoming the struggles that I have had to endure throughout my life.

So what changed in these ten years? I asked myself this question so often, to the point I even thought to use it as the title of this book. To find the answer, I have to listen to what my heart tells me: that my innocence was lost. I do want to make it very clear though: I think of 'innocence' as anything not backed by science. In the place of innocence, I believe that an awareness crafted from fire and iron was established.

My illusions were purged by the same fire and the iron that showed me that love and hate are both absolutes. Love loves and hate hates.

Over time, my view of the world has changed. Ten years ago, Cacha Pregos was my world. There were strange, short paths to other places. Today, I live in São Paulo, where I give lectures, courses and workshops. I've also worked in Minas Gerais, Salvador, Recife, Rio de Janeiro, Zug, Zurich, Yverdon-les-Bains. I still work in the latter three Swiss cities.

My opinions about religious people and mystics have now changed. I had no idea how deep rooted Catholic and Dogmatic beliefs were. I believe that many don't even realise their beliefs have such dogmatic roots.

They look to esotericism, spiritualism and Buddhism... They look at spiritual studies from an extremely Catholic point of view. These people say not to believe dogmatic Catholics, yet they interpret everything they study using the holy and demonic concepts imposed upon them by the Roman Catholic and Apostolic Church.

I don't believe this behaviour will allow us to move forward. There are so many unexplainable happenings; so many phenomena, truths and spiritual battles, many of which are viewed in much the same way as I can imagine they would have been in the Dark Ages.

Many things have changed over these past ten years! It started when my mother passed away, which coincided with the final stages of editing *An Apprentice's Journey*. In the morning, I was looking over the book, getting it ready to give to the editor and the printer. By the evening, during an out of body experience, I began to question my beliefs.

Those who have already read *An Apprentice's Journey* will understand what I'm talking about. In it, I describe my out of body experiences and encounters within the spiritual sphere; the space where we linger in-between incarnations.

During my out of body experiences to the astral plane, I accompanied people at the moment of their being born; those who were dying; those in comas.

When my mother passed away, I still hadn't completed the final draft of the book. Her death was such a profound experience, as was accompanying strangers. I, myself, have accompanied around two hundred cases and have studied a number of others over a four year period. Accompanying my mother threw my emotions into turmoil and made me question all my beliefs. The fact is that this event changed me greatly and prepared me for the changes I was to undergo.

Let me see how else I changed during this period.

People came and went...

There are some people who have lived with me, yet who are no longer in my life and who will not feature in this book.

There were many stages to my transformation, and the one that I felt most strongly was that which came only through growing up. The Catholic part of me made me think it so important for people to believe me. Now, I'm happy with them doubting me. My experience has taught me that what our eyes see, and our souls feel, can be changed if we are unable to explain what we have seen.

They say that, when we turn 40, we are given 'the keys to our shackles'. The truth is, I freed myself from these and, using my now free hands, I am able to write and better deliver myself.

Don't forget, I started this book when I was already part way through my journey, when I was somewhere between courage and fear.

*Chakras: the true story of a medium* is my story. Believe it if you can; if not, then doubt me. This is the first step to learning, and understanding, a different and not so common story.

So what didn't I change about myself? I am still a rebel. As the years went by, I never grew out of my rebelliousness. On the contrary, I continue to push the boundaries and still dare to say what I think; to do what I believe and live the way my conscious deems necessary.

I don't want gurus, I'm not looking for disciples, nor am I trying to start a religion. I was born to a man and a woman and I live in a world where it is necessary to learn to live together, in harmony, with both Yin and Yang. All I know is what happened to me. Everything I have learnt has been taken from my own body and my own experiences. Everything I write and talk about in my lectures and courses really happened. I'm not a theorist on spiritual matters. I don't study ancient texts.

When my chakras opened for the first time, I wasn't even aware of what a 'chakra' was. I had never heard of them. From that point on, however, I learnt to use them to read the Akashic records and to consciously astrally project myself to the spiritual plane of awareness. I want to tell you my story. If my story enlightens you, let the Universe thank me. You don't owe me anything; I'm not asking for anything in return. If it doesn't, let the Universe respond. It took me a long time to decide to write it.

At the age of 28, I preferred to hide my abilities completely.

The decision to take photos as my chakras opened, in order to document the event, was not mine. I agreed to it, but I was so afraid. I didn't know how people were going to react.

At the age of 30, I began to realise the importance of the photographic records.

At the age of 35, my life led me to show these photos to a few people. I didn't just show them these photos; rather I told them the secrets about how my chakras opened. Everyone who heard about me wanted to know where my knowledge and my clear thinking came from. I needed to reveal the name of my contact with the spiritual world and the Akashic records. Before this book, approximately forty people knew about my story.

At the age of 40, I understood that, for something to be secret, the person that keeps it secret must not know its relevance. A secret should either remain untold, or should be told to the world. A secret such as mine ought not to be kept by so few.

These reflections led me to write about the source of my knowledge.

As I've said, I'm not looking for disciples or supporters. I'm not starting a religion. That's not my *raison d'être*. If it were, I'd do it. But it's not. If fate had made starting a new religion as my life's purpose, I would do it. I was put on this Earth for another reason.

Science needs to understand the subtle body. Humanity needs to know about chakras. Man bathes because good hygiene is important in maintaining a healthy body. By that same token, man also needs to learn to cleanse his chakras.

Eastern religions have already shown the importance of chakras in the development of spirituality. I was brought into this world to show their importance in the development of a body that is more at peace in the way it thinks, feels and acts as a unit.

I'm starting a philosophical school. But if my life's purpose were to start a religion, I would do it.

With regards to this, my spirit friends told me:

*"Everyone has their own religion. Although religions institutionally go by different names, this institutionalisation only exists in social contact. The reality is that man looks at all religions and then develops a series of principles by which to live his life. Naturally, these will differ from person to person, as every one of us is unique. There is, therefore, no need to start new religions. Share your experience."*

I am Halu Gamashi. When I was born, my name was Mercia. I don't know the name by which I will go when I die. For as long as I am here, I'll continue to write and tell my stories, working in the way that I believe to be right, passing on the messages from the spiritual world, as well as those in relation to the earthly plane.

Through learning about the way in which the chakras open, I also learnt astrology, Cabala, Paracelsus' principle and the anatomy of the subtle body, amongst other things. During my out of body experiences to the astral world, I came across many people who are famous here on Earth. I came across people who are no longer remembered here. I got to know faceless people, who carry out special roles in the spirit world. However, learning about myself was the most important thing. If you don't know yourself, you will be unable to get to know or recognise anyone else.

In an attempt to get to know myself better, I will continue to write this book: *Chakras: the true story of a medium*. It has taken over my life, and I work on it both day and night.

I want you to enjoy this book, as well as the others that are soon to follow. Letters from my readers have made me push forward more than ever.

"Searching for people on the same wavelength as us is a right. Finding them is a pleasure."

# Part One

# Turunga

I was Turunga! My grandfather gave me the nickname. My name is (is?...) Mercia Celeste. Mercia was my mother's name and Celeste was my paternal grandmother's. It was the only thing it could be, although my grandmother had to bribe my mother with a gold bracelet for her to agree to it. She was so offended and thought it akin to blackmail. She didn't want to, and brought the discussion to a close by clearly stating what my name was going to be (was?...), Mercia Celeste. To avoid confusion throughout the book, I'll refer to each, respectively, using only their first name.

To stop the potential feud between the two, my grandfather decided that I was going to have a nickname: Turunga. My mother's family hated the name, Mercia Celeste, and thought I should just be called Mercia. That said, they thought the nickname, Turunga, was even worse!

All in all, Turunga was a sweet child! To be fair, are there any children that aren't? Oh, yes! There are! I've known a few over the years. Below are the traits that Turunga had:

- She was a chatterbox and always had a million and one questions about the world around her. She liked to run away and first did so when she was 3.
- She loved animals and so practically lived in the back garden.
- She was a loner, another reason she practically lived in the back garden.
- She was sick of the arguments at home, which was a third reason she practically lived in the back garden.

•She saw the spirits of those who had passed as if they were still among the living and so was sent to the back garden whenever she saw them at home. This was the only time that Turunga didn't want to go to the back garden... Her curiosity to know what they were saying and what they wanted had her captivated.

"Get out from under my feet, girl! Go outside and play!"

It took five or six years to discover my ability to see the spirits of those who had passed, as if they were still living, and to discover that I was able to see other people's auras. It was actually my nursery school teacher, Miss Olivia, who discovered it and it was she who told my mother. Before this, whenever they saw me fixated on people's shoulders, they thought me difficult to teach manners.

"What an obsession! The girl's always drawn to people's shoulders. It makes them uncomfortable! That's enough, Turunga! Celeste, you need to talk to the girl. Tell her to stop staring at passers-by!" shouted my grandfather to my grandmother; who would bark back: "You think I haven't already, Milton! Her mother's told her about it so many times. She just doesn't listen, so it's difficult to teach her manners."

As I write about this period in my life, I have to admit I struggle to recall every detail about what happened and who said what to whom. I was only four at the time, so my memories are a little unclear. Fortunately, where these events were seen as unusual, the stories have been told and retold to death by relatives.

When my grandfather passed away, I was 8 years old. My father never talked about our childhood, neither mine nor my brothers'. I don't know if he paid attention to us. He was self-centred and lived his life like he was the centre of the universe. Everyone else around him seemed to play less important, supporting roles in his life.

Anyway, back to Turunga...

When I was six, my family started to accept that I was not like other children! Back then, I was labelled as a medium. Nowadays, society offers plenty of other terms like: paranormal, sensitivity, 'schizophrenia' and the rest. We all judge each other on the way in which we behave and conform to what society deems to be normal.

I wonder if it was because of this that Turunga was afraid to be assessed. She could feel the weight of peoples' gazes upon her body like an iron bar. With her ability now clearly identified, she could feel her assessors' eyes giving her daggers.

Although the conclusions they came to were always different, the assessment was always the same. Turunga saw, and felt, the uncaring way they used to watch her walk. When she moved, some thought her walk to be quick and anxious. Others thought it sluggish and staggered. Turunga also had something unusual about her arms, which attracted attention - she was completely ambidextrous. This generated a great deal of comments, which always contained big and complicated words. Turunga knew that they weren't positive comments. She could tell from the tone of voice people used.

It was that tone used by adults when you're not allowed to have anything else to eat, or play in the rain or in the back garden.

Even though she didn't know what the 'diagnoses and hunches' were exactly, Turunga knew, from the tone of voice that she heard, the severity of the situation she was now in as a result of her arms, her legs and the constant staring.

The teachers at her school would whisper loudly so she could hear:

"Look, what a mad girl! She looks like a boy. She was born wrong. She should have been a boy."

"She doesn't like anything that little girls like. Little girls should like dolls. Whoever's seen a girl play football?!? She's sick; it's the only explanation!"

I wonder if it was because of this that Turunga tried to play behind the curtain. I don't know...

I wonder if it was because of this that Turunga enjoyed the company of animals in the back garden more than she did that of other people. I don't know...

Playing with animals or hiding behind the curtain can also be seen as odd.

To defend herself, she would look at the floor and shy away from people's gazes; looking for a way to escape the judgement. Turunga didn't know: everything she did meant something; was significant; was a determining factor; a character trait. These are theories thought up by academics who don't know much about people. People, who are different, like Turunga, usually attract more attention because they live in a small town. I don't know if you understand what I mean: the smaller a town or city, the more people want to appear like everyone else because being different is not usually welcomed. Otherwise, they discover their own personal and secret little quirks.

Turunga spent the first few years of her life like this. It was at this time that she was identified as a medium. My maternal grandmother, and one of my mother's aunts, were Kardec Spiritists and it was they that established her as a Medium.

What did Turunga think, and feel, about all this? Now that I don't know; I don't remember exactly. What I do remember from this period are the back gardens of the different houses I lived in.

In Jequié, the city where I was born, I lived in three houses: the first had a veranda at the front, with a rocking chair. I loved to play on the veranda. I remember Rex, a black dog, lying in the doorway. They say I practically used to live on top of him. That was, at least, up until the day I decided to take his bone and he bit my finger. So how did that end? 14 injections in my stomach! According to my grandmother, Rex ran away and only returned a month later, looking filled with regret. Everyone was so worried about the bite, which resulted in me having injections to prevent getting any nasty illnesses. Fortunately, I don't remember this.

The second house was very small and didn't have electric lights. My mother and grandmother used to clash. One day, they had a huge fight and we soon moved out. I'd like, at this point, to take the opportunity to provide you with some context, so that you are able to fully understand my story. My mother and father were very young, 16 and 19 respectively when I was born. The house was very dark. I remember a gas lamp and the box room where my parents used to sleep. It wasn't a house, it was a hostel. I close my eyes and remember the lamp on top of a little table.

"Don't touch that, Turunga, it's dangerous!"

"Turunga, if I see you near the lamp one more time, you're going to get it!"

I don't remember if they ever hit me, but I'll never forget that gas lamp!

The third house had a huge back garden. There were *pitanga* (a type of Brazilian fruit), avocados, peppers, lemons, chayotes and an orchard. Every house's back garden in Bahia grows peppers and lemons, or at least they used to. These would then be put into the dressings we would have with lunch. This was one of my grandfather's aunt's houses, either that or a second cousin's. I don't know, but we all used to call her auntie Alíria. She lived not far from my grandparents and always seemed to feel pity, embarrassment or shame – the latter being the most likely of the three – about the fact that my parents were living in a hostel with two small children. My brother was born around this time and we went to live with them. I loved the back garden. They didn't have chickens. Auntie Alíria's husband was a very stern man who didn't like creepy-crawlies. Despite that, I loved the back garden.

Bad memories aside, we returned to the first house. Later, we all went to live in another city, Santo Amaro da Purificação, where my second brother, my parent's third child, was born. This house was enormous, beautiful and had a huge back garden. We raised chickens, pigeons, dogs, cats and birds. It was almost a zoo!

"Turunga, who told you to wrap coloured ribbon around pigeons like that?"

"Ah! Janinho, please let me do it!"

"No! What madness; pieces of ribbon around the baby pigeons?!?"

Janinho was my uncle, from my father's side. Many years later, when he married, he ended up being called Jo by his wife. We all accepted the new nickname, but during this period, the time I'm talking about, Janinho was known as John Milton. We never called him by his actual name, only ever by his nicknames.

"Please, Janinho, please let me do it! Come on, don't you know anything?!"

"What do you mean, Turunga? What do you mean by that?"

"You don't know what you're talking about! You know yesterday, when you talked about pulling out my tooth?"

"Yes?"

"What did you say to me?"

"I said to pull out the wobbly tooth?"

"And then? Do you not remember anything else?"

"Spit it out, Turunga!"

"You said it wouldn't hurt and it did; it hurt a lot and still hurts now."

"If I'd told you it was going to hurt, you wouldn't have let me pull your tooth out!"

"So, if another becomes wobbly, I can't leave it because now I know it's going to hurt!"

\* \* \*

"Grandpa, how come you don't let me have chewing gum?"

"It's got sugar and it's bad for your teeth. Leave me to read the paper."

"Grandpa, do other sweets not have sugar?"

"They do... but it's different."

"The sugar's different?"

"No, chewing gum ruins your teeth. If you swallow it, it'll get stuck in your throat and you'll never be able to talk again!"

"Grandpa, nobody at school knows this and the teachers let all the children have chewing gum, except me because I'm not allowed."

"What the others do, or don't do, is of no interest to me. I don't want you to have chewing gum and that's the end of it!"

"What about the stickers you get with chewing gum; is that ok?"

"The stickers are fine; they aren't a problem!"

"But Grandpa, how can I get the stickers if you don't let me buy chewing gum?"

"Celeste, will you get this girl outta here? I want to read the paper!"

"Come on, Turunga, let's go to the back garden!"

\* \* \*

"Grandma, the 'Breadman's' arrived!"

"Has he really? Take him to the back garden to play with you."

The 'Breadman' is my spiritual mentor. I know this now; he is my friend, advisor and companion. I see him on a daily basis, but I'll talk more about this later. For Turunga, he was the 'Breadman'.

On the fifteenth of each month, my grandfather would distribute alms: bread, titbits, clothes... anyway, the house would be filled with beggars. My grandmother, although she agreed with it, thought it odd the way in which my grandfather performed charity. I thought these people were fun, each one being dressed funnier than the last, in strange clothes, different to those I usually saw at home.

When my mentor appeared in a blue tunic, I mistook him for one of those people who also dressed strangely. I nicknamed him, which wasn't uncommon to do in our family, 'The Breadman'.

"Grandma, the Breadman has come back!"

"Of course, Turunga, go and play with him in the back garden!"

"Breadman, how come you don't take the bread home with you? Do you have a house?"

"*One question at a time. What do you want to know first?*"

"Do you have a house?"

"*Yes, I do.*"

"Where is your house?"

"*The pretty place at the bottom of the garden!*"

"Will you take me there one day?"

"*If you like...*"

"And the bread, how come you don't take it? Do you not like bread?"

"*I like it when you give me bread; it makes me happy.*"

"Is it an act of kindness to give bread?"

"*Of course!*"

\* \* \*

"Grandma, is giving bread to the poor an act of charity, kindness or is it just alms?"

"What are you talking about, darling? What is this about?"

"Answer, grandma."

"Charity."

"Grandpa, is giving bread to the poor an act of charity, kindness or is it just alms?"

"It's something we all have to do, sweetheart! Those lucky enough to have everything share with those who aren't so fortunate."

"The Breadman said that it's an act of kindness."

"Breadman?"

"A man that comes here to see me."

"Celeste, what sort of talk is this? Who is this 'Breadman'?"

"It's one of her fantasies, Milton, an imaginary friend. I read an article published by a psychologist about this. Children have imaginary friends."

"I don't know, Celeste! Pay more attention to this story."

\* \* \*

"Breadman, are you my imaginary friend?"

*"Turunga, pay attention. I come here because we need to spend time together; a few minutes every day. Your grandparents love you dearly, but there are still things about you that they don't know. Later, later, they're going to know; be patient!"*

"Are you my imaginary friend?"

*"No, I am one of your friends that your family just hasn't met yet!"*

At the dinner table...

"You know, there are some things about me that you still don't know!"

"Celeste, Celeste!"

"I'm talking, mother, this girl is mad!"

"It's nothing; she just has a vivid imagination!"

\* \* \*

"Báu, do you think that my friend is imaginary?"

"The Breadman? I don't know, Turunga; ask mum."

"She says he is."

Báu is my aunt. They say that she's my grandparents' adopted daughter. I'm not sure. Báu always was and is, in my opinion, the best person in the family.

"What did he tell you?"

"He taught me to breathe."

"How?"

"He said it was like this: after we're born, we become scared, we fall to the ground, we misbehave. All of this together makes people forget how to truly breathe. He doesn't want me to forget."

"Turunga, have you told anyone else about this?"

"Just you."

"Keep this to yourself, Turunga. Don't tell anybody else. Ask him to come here when I'm at home."

* * *

"My aunt has asked for you to come back in the evening. At the moment, she's at school but she wants to get to know you."

*"Tell her I need the first few hours after sunrise to help you breathe. But tell her though, one of these days I'm going to come in the evening."*

I gave her his message; I don't remember what she said, nor do I remember if he kept his promise.

I eventually stopped talking about the Breadman. My grandmother talked to a specialist. He suggested not placing much importance on it, not to even pay much attention to it. The Breadman disappeared, just as he appeared. I'm grateful to the specialist, even though his prophecy of all spirits disappearing has not yet come to pass.

I don't have many memories of my parents from this time. There aren't even many photos of them in the scrapbook I made as a child. Well, there is one, where my mother was giving me a bath. In my scrapbook, I have photos of my grandmother, my grandfather and of Báu, my favourite aunt.

There are so many stories involving Turunga. Some of them I'd love to be able to write about; others I'd give anything to forget. That said, something that all these stories have in common is that I had learnt that being different isn't a good thing. It all boils down to who is in front of you, talking to you, judging you or even just forming an opinion about you.

Now I know I'm different. Now I know that no-one is the same, not really, especially those who either don't want or don't know how to conform to the hypnotic, and hypocritical, expectations society has for us.

But Turunga doesn't know any of this. One of Turunga's fears, perhaps even her biggest, was to drink milk, even though she loved it.

"Ah, I'm scared, grandma! Can I drink it? Or will it make me poorly?"

And so she tasted her delicious enemy. Afterwards she spent hours thinking, afraid she was going to become ill. This makes me think about the risks we run when the enemy is delicious. Aubergine is also bad for me, but I'm not running any risk. I never used to like it and still don't.

Turunga was born in the Sertão, a semi-arid region of Bahia, in the city of Jequié which has, over time, been nicknamed the "The City of the Sun". There is even a bus service in Jequié that has this name, or at least there used to be.

"The term *Sertaneja*, meaning from the Sertão, was born in a land of rams and ewes. Did you know that? They're related to you."

"Really, father?"

"Yes. The year you were born, many children died from tummy bugs, because of the heat. I know it was because of the heat, but somehow you survived. Both you and the goats!"

There are those who think that I have been either a little, or very, harsh towards my father in this story, but anyone who knows him, knows how much pleasure he would take in slandering and backstabbing the people around him. He referred to my mother as a "horse thief", for no reason other than she was born in Sergipe, Brazil's smallest state and, according to my father, anyone who comes from there is a "horse thief".

I'd like to apologise to the *Sergipanos*, the people from Sergipe, for my father!

Piauí, in the north-east of Brazil, was put on our family map when a nephew was born there. Him having been born there made my aunt feel uncomfortable.

I'd also like to apologise to the *Piauienses*, the people from Piauí, for my father!

Other groups of people he would insult were the Mineiros, who he referred to as: "lazy gits" and *Paulistas*, who he called "*Baianos*" that didn't turn out right".

I'd like to apologise, for my father.

"You and the goats are like brothers!"

"Really father?"

"Milton, don't play like this! You know that Turunga takes us seriously."

"She's a moron!"

"No she's not, Milton! She believes us."

How many times must my parents have quarrelled because of me? Whenever they did, Turunga felt as though she was the worst, and cruellest, of all God's creations.

"Now listen here, you foolish girl! The only reason me and your mum fought was because of you and you're not even my daughter!"

"No, dad? So whose am I?"

"Now listen here, ask your mother."

"Milton... Milton..." was her response.

Well, my father was referring to the intense heat of the summer, primarily in Sertão in Bahia. Most people are probably aware of the infant mortality rate in the north-east. It's lower now than it was, so they say... but back when Turunga was young, it couldn't have been higher.

The year I was born was plagued with disease. So many children lost their lives. I survived, but always showed signs of having an intolerance to milk. The doctors were slow to understand what the problem was. They diagnosed my intolerance as an intestinal infection. They all claimed to not know how it was that I had survived, until they discovered the intolerance and stopped giving me milk.

Around this time, my Uncle Mucio, my mum's brother, was an international pilot. Wherever he went, he would buy different brands of milk, trying in vain to find one that I could stomach. In the end, we just gave the different milks to the beggars that came round to the house on the fifteenth of each month. I started having arrowroot mixed with water. It's a type of flour and is very common in Bahia.

My paternal grandmother said that an angel advised her in a dream to give me arrowroot.

I stopped breast feeding 16 days after being born. No matter the type of milk they tried, it just didn't agree with me. One day, when I was aged about 6 or 7, my grandmother started to give me milk, a little bit at a time.

"You can't have too much. Remember, it could be fatal if you're not careful. Better to be safe than sorry."

Because of this, Turunga became almost phobic about drinking milk.

# A bit of background information on Bahia

There are those who say that Salvador is a city "that grows from the inside". The *Soteropolitanos* (the natives to Salvador) safeguard the secrets of the 'people'. I, in particular, agree with this statement and think it nice that they do this. Or at least it was. Fifteen years ago, I stopped living in Bahia. I'll go back for trips, as a tourist. Tourists just don't know a huge amount about the place they visit.

So, what were the 'people in Bahia' like?

Many used to write poetry and songs about the people from the area, but I'm going to give my thoughts.

The people in Bahia, as much as they would deny this, are very religious:

"I'm atheist, thank goodness!"

"That's your choice, but you never know! He may very well exist."

"It's not going to cost you anything to believe in it a little, is it?"

This is when they aren't religious conservatives. Being a religious conservative in Bahia is very interesting. This group is split into those people who opt for a single religion, and those who have at least two: Catholicism and Candomblé; Catholicism and Umbanda; Catholic and Protestant; political Catholicism and ritualistic Catholicism.

It's clear that the Roman Catholic and Apostolic Church is the most influential religious institution in Brazil. Why would it be different in Bahia? If Catholics in São Paulo, or in other states, knew what the religion is like in Bahia, they would, without doubt, be taken aback by the difference in the sermon, in the law or in the order.

I personally believe that Bahia is the place where Catholic influence is at its weakest and is least relevant. This is particularly the case, with the exception of a few landowners specialising in cacao, coffee and livestock, because it is such an impoverished State. Carrying out wedding ceremonies, baptisms and Mass was never something that was easy for the destitute to do; just as it wasn't for the Franciscans in the Middle Ages.

But Turunga didn't know anything about this. Turunga was born into a Republican State, where religion has a background in science and guides, education, politics and marriage.

When Turunga was around, literally everything needed to be run past the Priest, the minister, the *Babalorixa*, the President of the Centre, or the priestess who would receive the *Caboclo*, an ancestral indigenous Brazilian spirit, into herself. There were so many underhand dealings and agreements, including with the Priests and the ministers. The other dealings with religious people and groups were the same, but they were more discreet. It was never talked about and was kept secret by families. I think it is still like this, even today.

# Things they never knew about Turunga

"Celeste, Miss Olivia asked me to see her at school."

"I wonder why, Mercia?"

"I don't know; would you like to come with me?"

"Turunga, come here! Your teacher has asked us to go into school."

"She asked for my mother, grandma!"

"I'm also going. Do you know anything about it? Tell me, sweet heart."

"I don't know"

I didn't witness the conversation. I was only 4 at the time. When I got home from school:

"Turunga, come here. Take a look at that and draw what you see."

"I can't! Grandpa told me not to."

"So why did you do it at school?"

"The teacher, Miss Olivia, is in charge there. So there I can."

"Who told you this?"

"Both of them, grandma. I told grandpa that Miss Olivia didn't used to hit me when I would look at the colours around people. He said that she is the boss at school, so people will leave me alone if they think what I am doing is wrong."

"I'm confused, sweetheart. The colours around people? What's that?" my mother asked nervously.

"Don't you know how to see the colours around people then, mum?"

"Turunga, I'll be the one to ask the questions. Tell me about how you can see the colours around people." my grandmother instructed.

"I see in black and white and in colour. When I'm tired of looking at everything like everyone else, I make it so that I can see the different colours. Would you like to see?" Turunga replied.

"Is it her psychic eye, Celeste?" my mother asked.

"What do you see, Turunga?" my grandmother said, turning to me.

"Candyfloss, grandma."

"Candyfloss?" my grandmother repeated.

"It's lots of coloured balls. It's pretty!"

"Draw it for me so I can see."

It was like this that they started to learn "those things about me that they didn't know", just like my spirit friend had said they would. Talking of him... he played an important role in this episode:

*"Turunga, ask your mother to ask your grandmother Dulce for the books written by Chico Xavier. Did you make a note of the author's name?"*

And he repeated this, until it sunk in. I did as my spirit friend suggested. My mother shared the information with my paternal grandmother, Dulce.

"Chico Xavier? I have never heard this name. Is it another one of Turunga's imaginary friends? Do you remember what the specialist said? This teacher, Olivia, puts ideas in the girl's head. The Parish Priest says she's strange and only works at this school because the school owner is strange too. They are part of that religion, the one that talks to the dead, just like your mother and Alíria, Milton's cousin. You see? It was probably that teacher then that spoke about Chico Xavier and Turunga claims that it was the 'Breadman' who told her about him. Put it out of your mind."

But my mother couldn't forget. She even wrote a letter to her mother, recounting the story.

It is important to let the reader know that Turunga didn't fully understand what was going on. I only know what was said back then because people have since told me.

There were three big consequences to this tale:

•They took me out of school, in so doing, distancing me from

Miss Olivia and this was an irreparable loss!

•My grandmother told the whole story to the Parish Priest. He recommended she didn't let my mother read the book the Breadman had recommended and, as a result, this would limit her understanding of what was going on with Turunga. In the '60's, information on this topic was only accessible in Bahia through Chico Xavier. It's interesting that churches believe they have the right to decide what should, and should not, be read. It's like people don't have free will to be able to make the choice themselves.

•The war had started. On one side there was my grandmother, who wanted my mother to take me to the spiritualism centre she went to. On the other, there was my paternal grandmother who was convinced all of this was utter nonsense:

"The Priest said... The Priest thinks... The *Babalorixa* ordered..."

I remember how confusing all these fights were, but I never thought they were because of me. I think Turunga used to think: "A fight as big as this couldn't possibly have started because of someone as small as me."

This is what I think. If I'm honest though, I don't remember what all this was like for Turunga.

For Halu Gamashi, it helped to be distanced from religion and from religious powers.

When the fights ended, the truce started. Truces in my family are almost ironic. Is it also like this in your family? It was in Turunga's. Fights are followed by sarcasm. Up until the age of 9, Turunga used to prefer her family being sarcastic, despite not understanding why they were being so.

Turunga thought that the fights would end and that they would give way to smiles and laughter. She would laugh like the others and would bring a different type of irony to the table... innocence. She became part of something about which she didn't have any idea. She simply played her ironic role, whilst at the same time being out of place. It's interesting how ironic fate can be, isn't it?

In mistaking the smiles and the laughter as genuine, Turunga would innocently smile, and laugh, in her pure, childish way.

"They still like me!" she thought.

"Bloody Church nut, go and get me a *cabidela* chicken!" my grandfather would bark at my grandmother.

"Atheist heretic, ask properly otherwise I'm not going to do it!" my grandmother used to reply.

"Your mother, Mercia, is a disorganised, madwoman!" my father would say to my mother.

"Your family is unhappy!" she would respond.

Nowadays, this is how I see my family: my grandfather is an atheist communist; my grandmother is a Catholic fanatic; my father is a capitalist and opportunist; my mother is an orphan in search of a home. Finally, Turunga is a girl whose behaviour, and talents, were not seen as normal and whose obliviousness to the problems in her family complicated her life no end.

* * *

"Serginho, this is Turunga! Go and play together."

Turunga went.

"*Hi, I'm Mauro. What's your name?*"

"I'm Turunga."

"*Ask my mother to sing happy birthday to me. I'm ok. Ask her not to cry. It wasn't her fault. Speak to her.*"

"Why don't you ask her yourself?"

"*She can't hear or see me.*"

"But why not?"

"*Speak to her, please. What's stopping you?*"

"Aunt Miriam, Mauro is asking for you to sing happy birthday to him. He says he's ok."

"What did you say, sweetheart?" Aunt Miriam replied.

"He's ok! He also said that it wasn't your fault."

The thud from Aunt Miriam fainting broke the deafening silence! I looked from my mother to my father, both of whom had a disbelieving look on their face. I smiled, to see if the look they were giving me was a joke. It wasn't!

"Get your coat, now! We'll talk when we get home!" my father barked.

"Wait, Milton, let me talk to her!" my mother begged.

"Miriam, the child is an ungrateful wretch. She must have heard it said somewhere and..." he hissed at her.

"Where, Milton? Have you said anything to her? Has anyone?" my mother shrieked at him.

"Auntie Miriam, Mauro told me!" Turunga interrupted.

"Shut your mouth, you wretched girl! Can't you see that Miriam is suffering? Come on, Mercia, we're leaving. I can't take it any more from her." my father ordered.

I'd already taken my fair share of beating and clips round the ear but, on that day, Turunga received a beating like no other! When we got into the car, my scalp was so sore from where my father had pulled at my hair.

"Calm down, Milton! Wait, it's not her fault, my mother told me!" my mother screamed.

"Don't get involved, woman! You and your tramp mother; living as husband and wife with that bike of a man. You're just like her. They should never have been granted the right to marry in a church, or been given that marriage certificate!" my father roared.

"Milton, that's enough! One thing has absolutely nothing to do with the other!" my mother screamed again.

"Shut your mouth! You have no idea how much humiliation I've endured from friends and colleagues!" he snarled.

He looked at me in the rear-view mirror, took his hands off the steering wheel and slapped me over and over again, until I fell unconscious.

Recalling this memory actually reminds me of another:

"I have never hit my children; I'm not a violent man and I don't believe it's the answer." our 'noble Milton' used to lie to his friends about the way in which he was bringing us up.

"Oh! Milton, I don't know, the occasional slap on the ass isn't going to hurt." his friend retorted.

"No! Under no circumstances! I'm completely against it!" the liar insisted.

I was only 7 years old when this happened.

"*Hey, could you ring the doorbell for that house there!*"

"Me?"

"*Yes girl, you! Ring that doorbell there!*"

Turunga was stood by the door of the house she was living in Salvador. The house belonged to one of her father's aunts.

"Why don't you just walk up the steps and ring the doorbell, sir?"

"*I can't. Do it for me, please!*"

I looked at the old man and thought: he really isn't capable of walking up the steps. He's so old, poor man!

"Are you ill?"

"*That I am, child. I'm so very ill. Please, ring it for me. My daughter lives there.*"

"She moved here last week and she never spoke to me or to anyone in my family." I answered.

"*Ring the doorbell. Her name is Edith, but I call her Didi.*"

I looked at him and thought about it for a second, before deciding to help. Alas, this was one of the life-lessons I had been raised with: show respect to, and help, your elders whenever you can.

My father's aunt's house had a cement bank on the small veranda. A wall separated the two houses. I climbed on the bank, on the wall and I rang the doorbell.

"Who's there?" Didi called from inside.

"You father is here to see you, Edith. He is in the street. He asked me to ring your doorbell, because he isn't able to climb the steps." Turunga replied.

"Where is he then, child?" she asked me.

"Look at him there, Edith!" I replied, pointing.

"Where? Where is my father? What sort of talk is this?" she asked me again.

"*Didi, it's me. Forgive me. Please open the door and let me in; forgive me, Didi.*"

"There, Edith. He calls you Didi. He is begging forgiveness and..."

"Child, how do you know my name? My nickname? And who told you about my father?"

In that moment, I understood. Turunga had seen, and was talking to, spirits again.

"Oh my God, Edith! My father is going to kill me. I'm sorry, I didn't know... I only wanted to help, for the love of God, Edith..."

"Calm down, sweetheart! I'm not going to do anything to harm you."

My whole body was shaking.

*"Child, can you call Didi again?"* asked the old man repeatedly.

"Shut your mouth. You'll get me into trouble. Just go! Enter the gates of St Peter. That is where you belong." Turunga retorted.

Edith had gone back inside the house and returned with a glass of water for me.

"I don't want it, Edith." I told her.

Turunga ran home and lay on the sofa.

"What's wrong, Turunga?" Mezé asked me.

"For the love of God, Mezé, don't say a word!" Mezé is Maria José's nickname. She came from the countryside when she was still a baby to live with my auntie. I grew up with her and she ended up becoming part of the family.

"What's happened?"

"Don't go out the door, Mezé, don't you go out!"

She went out and came back white as a ghost, looking very nervous.

"Edith, our neighbour, wants to talk to your mother. What did you do, Turunga?"

Mezé was right: above all, Turunga was a versatile girl. She was creative and never missed out on the chance to show off her art, or do pranks to entertain herself. Playing ball sports, hopscotch, hot potato and marbles... as well as sticking adhesive tape to the doorbells on other houses, pouring grease on people's porches and houses. Of all the pranks she pulled, there is one that is worthy of being remembered. Turunga ended up even going as far as including the Afro-Catholic-Religion-Candomblé mix found in Bahia in the prank.

Turunga and her brothers had a white cat who was given the

unimaginative name: Branquinha (Snowflake). She was originally called Mimi but then, after we found the neighbour's cat had the same name, my brothers and I changed its name to Branquinha, who ended up birthing a number of kittens. Branquinha eventually passed away after an episode of flystrike, where maggots ravished her poor body.

The day before, Ms Cabeluda complained to Turunga's mother about a particular 'prank' Turunga hadn't actually taken part in. It wasn't true, but Turunga's mother believed the whole story and Turunga was punished.

"Mum, she is lying. It wasn't me!"

"Nonsense! So here is what we are going to do. Tonight you'll go to bed without watching TV, without playing football. You're grounded and will go to bed early."

When the sun came up, Branquinha passed away. Let's cry, pray and bury her.

"Bring the candle and the phosphorus, we'll put her in a shoe box..."

"I have an idea." Turunga announced. "We don't have anywhere to bury Branquinha. Let's leave her on Ms Cabeluda's porch. You, bro, ring the doorbell and run."

"And you?" my brother asked me.

"I'll stay here on the wall to see if she opens the door or window. If she does, then I'll give you a signal and then you wait for her to go back inside."

"What time are we going to do this?" he asked.

"We'll wait until mum goes to school for the kids!"

The children she meant were the two youngest. By now, Turunga's mother had four children and Turunga was the eldest.

It all went as planned. That day, my brother almost took a dirty drop in his rush not to be 'caught' by Ms Cabeluda.

Turunga would never have imagined the reaction that followed. The neighbour opened the door and shouted. She shouted so much. At the end, she claimed:

"This is sorcery! Sorcery I tell you! My son was taken on by the energy company 'Petrobras'. She's jealous because my son was accepted and the son of a certain person wasn't!"

By 'certain person' she meant the other neighbour, a woman with whom Ms Cabeluda had lost no love.

"Run Bibi, call Mãe Olga do Beco. Call her to break this spell!"

There was no-one else other than Mãe Olga do Beco. Half an hour later she was cleaning Ms Cabeluda's door, singing and dancing as she worked: she and other people.

"It's precisely this, Cabeluda! This is witchcraft!"

Me and my brother were wetting ourselves laughing from the small veranda... or at least we were up until we saw our mother returning home with our younger brothers.

"Quick! Run inside!" Turunga said.

"It's your fault, did you not see? You did this, don't try and spin your web of deceit!" my brother whispered.

"Really? You had just as much fun as me! You're still laughing now!"

"Cover for me!" Turunga's brother barked.

Turunga still heard the conversation.

"Olga and Cabeluda, what happened?"

"Ah! Mercia, it's good that your children are just that. Behold the Devil's envy!"

My mother looked at 'the Devil's envy' and recognised the cat in the old shoebox.

"I'll see you later, Olga, I'm going home!" my mother said sternly.

* * *

"I swear, Mezé, it wasn't me this time; I swear!" I cried.

"The new neighbour wants to talk to your mother." Mezé replied.

This chapter of my life ended with my mother telling the neighbour that I saw the spirits of those who had passed, as if they were still among the living, and that this wasn't the first time that this had happened.

"Mercia, I believe in this! The girl couldn't be making this up.

She was even able to tell me what my nickname was when I was a child! Take her to the centre, otherwise you and she will suffer greatly!" Edith said.

"But, Edith, her father doesn't want this!" my mother replied.

# Mãe Helena

Knee, foot, pedal, the floor is the sky, speed...

"Get out of the way, move! Here I come; I'm going to win the prize! I won! I won!"

Turunga let the bike fall to the floor. Cries and chants flooded the streets.

"Mãe Helena, Mãe Helena, guess who won the bike race?"

"You managed to sort everything out?" Mãe Helena asked me.

"Mr Luiz from the bar had a spare wheel lying around and it worked, Mãe Helena! And Curió fitted the brake using a wire. I didn't even need to use the brake during the race though; I didn't need to!"

"That's great, darling; now go and wash. Your family is coming today. They want to see you!"

"But later on, they're going to go and I'll stay, right?"

"Go and wash, and don't forget about *maionga*, a special bath of herbs."

"Mãe Helena, will we have to sing?"

"Yes, to summon the ancient forces."

Mãe Helena was a healer and knew everything about the different energies in nature, the cure and disease, as well as how to cast out illness.

"You need to know, little one. Ancient forces reside within you. You have Indian blood inside you. I don't think this strength comes from Brazil. Your gifts come from a time long ago. They are not from this place."

"What gifts, Mãe Helena?"

If I'm honest, Turunga used to ask questions for the sake of asking questions. She used to want to keep the conversation going and dreamt about finding the love of that old black woman who gave her back her life and, also, the strength to carry on living her life. Mãe Helena used to smoke a pleasant smelling cigar before going to sleep.

"Pay attention, girl. I'm going to tell you a legend."

"What's that?"

"Once upon a time, there was a Queen. You know what a Queen is, don't you?"

"I think so, but I'm not sure. I've never seen one; only ever heard about them in the stories."

"This Queen had a son who was very poorly, bless his heart. Obviously, knowing how much he was suffering was unbearable for her and so she asked God to cure his illness. The Queen didn't know that his illness didn't have a cure, that the only person who could cure the illness was actually her son... her little Prince."

"So God didn't cure my illness? I cured myself?"

"I hope so. You are very intelligent, sweetheart. My only hope is that you may follow your path. Now, pay attention."

"The Queen prayed to God and, where God could see the purity in the Queen's heart, he sent a cure to the child. As a result, the Prince spent six months being poorly and another six months being healthy. Time went by and the Queen couldn't understand why it was like this. When the little Prince was healthy, he was handsome, strong and elegant. In the six months where he was poorly, he grew weak, sad and his body became plagued with injuries. Not a day went by when he didn't pray and ask God to help him understand why all this was happening to him. To make the situation even worse, when the Prince was healthy, the Kingdom flourished. Plants grew, animals became fat. Life was good. But when he was poorly, the animals also became ill, plants wilted and died and the clean rivers grew dirty. Life was horrible and the Kingdom was sad. Having seen the tears that the Queen was crying, God sent her an answer... wisdom in corporeal form, as another child. When she found out she was pregnant, the Queen was so happy and, when the new Prince was born, the whole Kingdom came to see him."

"Everyone wanted to know if he, like the first Prince, had been born poorly. Luckily, he wasn't. They saw that he was a gorgeous baby and was happy and smart. But, over time, the young Prince didn't learn to walk. No matter how hard he tried, he just couldn't stand up and stay stood up. Instead, he dragged himself around, on the floor, whenever he wanted to move."

"What's wrong, sweetheart? Is the story making you sad?"

"The Princes are like me, aren't they, Mãe Helena?"

"Yes. You were like this when you came here."

"I was like this a long time ago, years ago! I was completely unable to walk!"

"I know; Humberto told me! Anyway, pay attention to the rest of the story: The Prince had no desire to walk. Instead, he dragged himself through the garden, towards the rivers. When he learnt to swim, he picked it up so quickly. Seeing him swim in the rivers was something quite special, as he did it so beautifully. There was no-one in the Kingdom who learnt to swim faster than he did."

"Mãe Helena, were there swimming pools in the Kingdom?"

"No. None at all. Just rivers."

"Did you know that I've also won two swimming competitions? I even got a medal! I was once also going to get a trophy, but the swimming teacher gave it to the club instead. But it wasn't the club that won it, it was me! I even have the photo at grandma's house."

"You see? You're starting to understand where I'm going with this story."

"Where are you going with the story, Mãe Helena?"

"Don't ask just yet. Just listen to the rest of the story and you'll see."

"One day, the young Prince just stood up and started walking and running. He showed the Queen, and everyone else he was able to prove that he didn't have a problem; to prove that he wasn't sick. Overnight, the Prince turned into a wise man. He became so very intelligent and knew everything about everything. It was like he had become a teacher, and a doctor, at the same time. His name was

Bessem. When the Queen saw how smart the Prince had become, she asked to speak to him. 'Bessem, why is your brother, Omolu, forever changing between being healthy and then becoming poorly again?' 'Mother, he is important! Omolu is strong and so very loved by God. His body holds all the world's illnesses and cures. God sent me here to study and learn the secrets of medicine. I'm here to understand why there are those patients who want to continue as they are.'

'Whenever I find illness I call Omolu, who then gives them the cure that strips the illness from their body.'"

"And just like that, Bessem discovered the secrets of the plants that were dying and, with Omolu's help, he cured them. He discovered the secrets of the animals that were losing weight and, again, with the help of his brother, Omolu, he cured them. From time to time, they would come across people who were ill and they would do the same. Because of the work the two princes did, there was never again sickness, or disease, in the Kingdom. Omolu cast out the illness that had plagued the Prince, which meant that he never again suffered from disease. They then lived happily ever after, until the end of their days."

"Are legends and stories the same thing?"

"More or less. What did you think of it?"

"I liked it!"

"Now, we need to try and work out the secret. Why do you think you were so ill; do you have any ideas?"

"Everyone thinks something different, but it was you who cured me!"

"I didn't, sweetheart. It was the Orishas who helped me find a cure for you. They are the different types of energy out there in nature."

Mãe Helena was a Candomblé nonconformist. She disagreed with some of the practices, and beliefs, based on 'traditional Candomblé' and she shut herself away from them. She became a healer and learnt about different types of energy: balanced and unbalanced. She learnt about what causes it and also consequences associated with it. What's more, Mãe Helena knew how to unblock energy channels.

But Turunga didn't know any of this. Her illness appeared 'overnight' and, inexplicably, she found herself unable to walk. To begin with, the doctors diagnosed the illness as rheumatic fever, even though Turunga hadn't had a temperature. But, using a blood test, they detected the presence of Beta haemolytic streptococci, a bacteria responsible for causing rheumatic fever.

I stayed in the hospital, taking antibiotics such as penicillin and painkillers, etc. They ran tests and eventually decided to change the diagnosis they had originally given me. They now thought the condition to be atypical rheumatic fever. It was strange, different to what they would normally have expected. Tests, money, injections and Turunga worsened with every day that passed. They called a specialist and sent the blood tests away to São Paulo and Rio de Janeiro, only to get back results similar to those given by the other doctors.

"I'm not going to buy a wheelchair, I'm not! If I buy it then I have to admit, and accept, that my daughter is a cripple." I heard my father say.

When I heard that, it actually made me like him that day. It was nice to hear something so nice leave his lips, given it was such a rare occurrence.

At night, Turunga had night terrors and would wake up afraid and in floods of tears. It was difficult to go to school and it added work for the teachers. In the beginning, 'everything was ok, everyone was kind'. Over time, however, the kindness disappeared and Turunga felt herself to be a burden to everyone around her and felt increasingly uncomfortable in her own skin.

"Mercia, please, I need to say something to you. You need to look for Orishas. I have been a doctor now for many years and there is something wrong with your daughter's profile. Look for other ways to help Turunga. I wouldn't be able to forgive myself if I didn't say this to you. If she carries on like this I'm afraid this girl won't last the month. Her liver isn't able to withstand this much penicillin. She's now been on Benzetacil every week for two years, yet there is still no difference. She isn't responding the way the doctors thought and the way we had hoped she would."

"Would you speak to my husband?" my mother replied.

And so he did. He spoke with Turunga's father and with the two mother-in-laws. He had even spoken to Turunga. It was such a long road before meeting Mãe Helena.

It all started with one of my grandmother's dreams. My grandmother and her dreams! First of all it was the arrowroot, the flour they gave me as a child. My grandmother is so Catholic, so believes that any dreams like this have been brought to her by 'an angel'. This is the type of thing that my grandmother says, using her own special 'language'.

After thinking about this, I understood…that every settler, every invader in history forced his language on the peoples they conquered. Through language, we are unable to understand when someone is talking about the same thing as us, just using different words and expressions. From this, we develop precepts, and make incorrect assumptions, and develop the attitude that 'my truth is the only truth'.

But Turunga didn't know anything about this! Turunga created Halu Gamashi and allowed her to enter into her life, so that she might reflect in the present the way Turunga learned in the past. I'm convinced that Turunga had Halu Gamashi hidden somewhere deep inside her and the two of them hid deep within Mercia Celeste.

Turunga wanted to be able to walk again. She wanted to stop the pills and the potions but, above all, she wanted to put a stop to being a 'charity case' to everyone around her and go back to being independent.

Whilst everyone discussed whether or not Turunga should be taken to the Orishas she remembered that, three years prior, she climbed the cashew trees and sold cashew nuts to tourists in the hippy village of Arembepe.

Arembepe is a beach, located not far from Salvador, where Turunga's family used to spend the summer. Turunga used to look at her deadened legs and thin, weak arms and would think: "I wonder if I still have the strength to be able to push the donkey to the river to find water in the *Pau*, a small, crystal clear stream".

Around this time, at the end of the 1960's, running water and electricity were not something that was present in Arembepe. The beach had been taken over by hippies. They said that it was a very special place. They used to talk about flying saucers, intergalactic commanders and peaceful invaders that had come from God only knows where, to save Planet Earth from who knows what!

But Turunga didn't understand any of this!

How could she if she was totally taken aback by the beauty of the virgin sea and wildness in Arembepe? She adored the white beaches, filled with *graucas* – small crustaceans that parade along the sand, in search of the mess left in the wake of local children who have enjoyed a day at the beach.

The hippies would say that they needed to run around naked, remove their clothes and let their hair down.

Turunga wasn't even there. Even as a child, she didn't feel the need to strip off, to be able to enjoy the beauty and purity. For her, it made no difference whether she was dressed or not; the beauty was still there to behold.

Fishing for the silvery *xixarro* with Ms Betinha's and Ms Paixão's children; eating some of the nuts and selling others to tourists, who didn't have time to fish and who, instead, played in the sea. They were more worried about the flying saucers that would come in and bring with them the special nectars on which to feast.

Turunga ate the freshly caught *xixarros* with cashew nuts – the same ones she had been selling to the tourists. She would go back to their homes and 'scavenge' the nuts that lay abandoned in the same back gardens where the tourists would relax and get together to net-work.

Turunga scavenged the nuts in exchange for a pittance for having tidied the garden.

She was sat on the sandbanks waiting for that sweet and salty sea breeze that always passed at the end of the day. She ate the fish and the nuts, staring at the miracle of the water. She watched the waves swell and break upon the shore, against Turunga's feet, then retreat back to the ocean as fast as they had appeared. There were stunning seashells, and many other invisible living creatures that Turunga could see, but about which she would not breathe a word to anyone for fear of being hit, or bringing shame upon the family and being left behind.

"Turunga, Turunga, what are you thinking about sweetheart?"

"I'm just thinking back to Arembepe, grandma! Where is my mother?"

"We are getting ready for a meeting. I've had one of my dreams. I dreamt about a man I've never met. All I know is that he is real and that he is outside! We were able to contact him. It's a long story, but his name is Humberto and he wants you to listen in to the whole conversation."

"But why, grandma? Is he another doctor?"

"No! Well, what I mean is that he isn't a doctor like the others."

"Grandma, you're just waffling!"

"Turunga, pay attention! We're going to make a very important decision and I don't understand why Humberto insists on you being present."

"It's ok, grandma!"

"Let's get you in the bath whilst your father makes his way home from work."

Taking a bath was very difficult though, to be fair, everything I did was. My mother and grandmother used to carry me to the bathroom. There was the chair, the shower and soap waiting for me in there.

"Humberto, please don't be offended by this. You're here of your own free will to help my daughter..." my mother started to say.

"I'm sorry to cut across you... It's true, I am here to help you and your daughter, but that is not the main reason I am here. I'm here because someone once did this for me. It opened my eyes and helped to disillusion me and showed me how to help my wife."

Humberto spoke a bit about his wife. Her situation had been similar to mine. She became ill. The doctors she went to were unable to produce a diagnosis for her. They were unable to cure her. It was almost the same as what was happening to me!

"Mr Humberto, what is your wife's name?" I asked.

"Gloria; what about yours?"

"Turunga. Well, actually, Turunga is a nickname. My real name is Mercia Celeste, but no-one calls me this... except my maternal grandmother, but I hardly ever see her."

I had started to tell him about my grandmother's travels when they interrupted me.

"Turunga, allow him to speak!"

He looked at me and, in that moment, I was sure he would have preferred to speak to me.

"I can't say for definite if Turunga needs help from the Orishas or not. I don't have enough knowledge to confirm this, but believe me when I say that we all need to know, and understand, about the owners of this planet."

"Owners of this planet?" my father asked, sounding sarcastic as always.

"You don't know about them? What are the Orishas to you?"

"The madness of ignorant people." responded my 'wise' father.

"How long have you lived alongside this culture? What do you know about it? Do you know anything about the African tribes and the rich culture they hide from those who do not wish to learn about it?"

"Yes, well, erm..."

"Milton, this reminds me of those people who know a lot about a lot of things, but who have not experienced them personally. I'm not a madman, nor am I ignorant. However, you sir, are both mad and ignorant! You stand there, freely offending someone who can help your daughter. I haven't left the hospital because of my belief."

I loved Mr Humberto. "Well said, well said!" Turunga silently shouted.

"Milton, bite your tongue or leave!" barked the supreme authority. My grandmother always knew how to put him in his place when she had run out of patience with him.

"Mr Humberto, what will they do to my granddaughter? Please forgive so many questions; we have just heard so much about this culture; some of it quite dark!"

"You are quite right, Celeste! When they said about me taking my wife to see the Orishas, I had the same concerns, for the same reasons that you now have. Yet I didn't have these same concerns when I took her to see doctors. Why is that? They are all knowledgeable. They all seek to cure ailments. They are all trained scientists. From my experiences with the Orishas, I have come to realise that conventional doctors do not know everything, quite the contrary in fact." Mr Humberto explained.

"This explanation was perfect. No-one ever showed any concern when the doctors came to take my blood, or run tests, or pump me full of drugs that would have horrific side-effects. I have been going through this for two years." I thought to myself.

Mr Humberto drank his drink to give them chance to mull over this most recent notion.

"The things they say, or rather, the untrue things they say about the Orishas have no real grounding; much the same way any exaggerations about traditional medicine have no real grounding. Turunga is proof of this. How long has the poor girl been like this?" Mr Humberto asked.

"Roughly two years." my father said.

"Her whole life, Mr Humberto." my mother said, breaking the silence.

"What's this, Mercia? Have you lost your senses?" the 'wise man' said.

"That's enough, Milton! I'm going to talk! I'm going to say my piece! I am her mother and I am going to say what I have to say!"

"Milton, please don't be offended by what I'm saying but, from what I can see, you like to accuse the people around you of being mad." Mr Humberto stated.

I remember my grandmother shooting my father with her sharp look. My grandmother had this look that would speak volumes. To this day, I've never met anyone who could give a look quite like hers! And when she gave these looks, you could 'hear' what her gaze was saying.

"There has always been so much going on in her life, Humberto. She was born with an intestinal infection, or possibly an atypical allergy. Atypical is a word that seems to accompany every diagnosis Turunga is given. It has been like this ever since she was little." my mother added.

"Mr Humberto, I see the spirits of the dead as though they were still alive!"

Turunga also possessed an atypical courage, in the sense that, although she would not bring the topic up herself, she would not shy away when her abilities were mentioned. She didn't look at anyone. She just spoke and hoped.

"What's that, Turunga? Explain it to me again, in more detail!" he whispered to me.

"Didn't I say that she shouldn't be here?" my father interrupted.

My grandmother gave my father another glare.

"It's true, Mr Humberto, I do!" I told him some of my stories. Mr Humberto smiled a lot and cried a little.

"How ignorant we all are! And I'm also including the responsibility that Afro-Brazilian people have, with regards to the prejudice other people have about their culture and practices. They are the first to hide secrets about their knowledge. They are also the first to recount stories that never happened to them. When you understand more about Candomblé, you'll see that I'm right..."

"So then, Mr Humberto, what people say about Candomblé isn't the truth?" my grandmother asked curiously.

"White people are deceptive with regards to black culture, in particular, to their religion…" Mr Humberto explained.

"…The blacks don't want the whites anywhere near them, so they don't get to shed any light on their way of life and they leave people to come up with their own assumptions."

"Why?" the 'Wiseman' asked, this time with more humility.

"It's a way of protecting their knowledge. If people don't place much importance on it; if they think of it as ignorance or madness, as you said, they keep the undesirables at bay and they are left untainted."

"My God, father!" Turunga shouted this time, not so silently. She let a small smile escape. It was small, but irritating...

"Once, Mr Humberto, our cleaner was in one of these houses and she told me everything. The people there, priests, lords, holy men; they cut you up and bleed you dry. They say that once you go in, you can't get out; otherwise you die."

"Forgive me, Celeste! But your cleaner must have gone to a place where there were no traces of the Orishas. There are so many people out there who use the name of the Orishas to blackmail, exploit and frighten people. People don't behave like this in an Orisha's house. We would have to undertake a long journey to meet with these people. You will bear witness to how difficult it will be for me to summon an emergency meeting with them. The blacks intend to study ritualistic sciences and share the knowledge with those who wish to study, in-depth, all aspects of their magic."

"Are they magic?" the 'Wiseman' asked, emerging from the shadows once more.

Mr Humberto ignored him and continued:

"Afro-Brazilian knowledge can be used to cure because it looks at health in an ethical way. To understand what I am talking about, you need to learn to live with them. In Turunga's case, I'm going to have to go before you. I'm going to need to speak at length, in order to get them to grant an audience."

"It's like this, is it?" asked my father, the 'Oracle'.

"It is, Milton! An Orisha's house is not like an asylum, or a prison, rather it is not open to the public, and therefore an appointment is needed."

This time, Turunga openly laughed.

* * *

I arrived at Mãe Helena's house. It was a hovel, right in the heart of the woods. There was no running water, no electricity, nothing at all that could be called a luxury. It was in the outskirts of Massaranduba, a poor district in Salvador.

I never forgot that day. She was sat on the porch. Her closest neighbour was just over a mile away. Wooden and hovel, bench, coal, brick and smell of coffee all rushed up from the smoking pot, filling our noses. I wonder if the smell of the coffee ever aided, or impeded, our ability to see. I can't speak for my family, but I loved it all.

"Is it here, Mr Humberto, the Orisha's house?"

"Milton, it would be far more helpful if your questions had more substance to them!"

Mãe Helena was sat on her wooden chair. It was the only

chair she owned. She stood up and came over to me. She looked at each member of my family, one by one, and held her gaze only when her eyes reached my mother. At last, she spoke:

"It's serious! Leave her here. Come back in forty days." she instructed.

"What?" my father piped up. "No, of course not!"

"Then you'll take her far away from me to die!" Mãe Helena hissed.

"Mãe Helena, I am her grandmother. I don't know what to say to you, so please forgive me if my questions offend you in any way, but..."

"You can ask me whatever you like, but my work is a relation-ship of trust. I'm not going to be able to explain what's happening with Turunga in just a mere day or two. It took more than twenty years for me to understand it myself. I started to study energy when I was 18. At the age of 38, I became an Ialorixa, a priestess. At 45, I disagreed with some things so distanced myself from it. I distanced myself from Candomblé, not from the Orishas. I have now turned 80. To be honest, I've been working with the elements in nature for more than 60 years. Do you have any idea how long it would take me to be able to teach you everything I have learnt in a way that you would understand?"

"Do you think my daughter can get better?" my mother asked.

"She's healthy. She isn't sick! What she needs is to know how to channel the energies within her. They are so strong. I've never seen a white person with such power! Even if she were black, what I see in her is rare. If she doesn't learn how to channel these energies, she'll die."

"If my daughter isn't sick, why does she need all these reme-dies?" asked the 'sarcastic Wiseman'.

"Do you see the word 'drugstore' floating anywhere around here?"

"No... but..."

"Do you see the word 'drugstore' floating anywhere around here?" she repeated sternly. "You are going to need to make a lot of changes or else you will lose your entire family."

All of Mãe Helena's prophecies have come to pass, including this one.

"They're going to die?" Milton asked her.

"No. You are going to die for them. You are an arrogant man who has nothing better to do than mock those around you."

"Shut up, Milton! So, Mãe Helena, how can we help you do what is needed?"

"By leaving" Mãe Helena retorted laconically.

"Turunga, you're listening to all this. I now understand why Humberto insisted so much on you being present right from the word go. Would you like to stay, sweetheart?"

"I want to, mum! I want to stay with Mãe Helena."

"Very well, stay."

"I think that I can decide, don't you?" the fake humility my father displayed reminded me of a small child having a tantrum.

"No, no you cannot, Milton." retorted my mother. "She's entitled to decide where she wants to live and die. It isn't as if the doctors know what to do."

"Mãe Helena knows what to do, mum, I know she does." I said, cutting across my mother.

Mãe Helena looked at me, exhaled deeply, slowly and deeply. She strode up to the door of the hovel and walked inside. She came back carrying a kind of rattle made of wood and metal and spoke to me authoritatively.

"When you were born, could you walk?" she asked as she shook the *adjá*, a kind of rattle, and my body tingled from head to toe. "I would like you to answer my question." She went back to shaking the *adjá* and repeated the question: "When you were born, could you walk?"

"Yes, Mãe Helena!"

"Well then, walk. Go and sit on that step there!"

Suddenly, she started to talk in a strange language to Turunga. Halu Gamashi will be able to go into more detail about this. Mãe Helena spoke to Turunga in an African dialect, in the language of the Orishas.

Turunga stood up and did as she was told, in the way she was commanded by Mãe Helena, whilst she had shaken the *adjá*. Now, for those of you out there wondering what in God's name an *adjá* is, it is a tool that is used to make a sound that causes our energies to become more pure, more potent.

The gasp was universal. Even Mr Humberto was open-mouthed. My father's eyes seemed to almost pop out, like they were on stalks. Even my grandmother was speechless. And what about Turunga?

Turunga smiled. She was calm and, as incredible as it sounds, was not surprised.

There were thirty days between now and the day of the bike race. Thirty days of fighting. Believe it if you can, otherwise, open yourself through the benefit of the doubt.

* * *

I washed myself in a bath of herbs. I chanted special prayers and went to the vegetable garden in front of Mãe Helena's. Although we were in the woods, there was a distance of two kilometres between her house and the street, so we could listen to the sound of the car approaching.

"Child, you need to answer any question they may ask you. Be patient with your family, in particular with your father. When you grow up, you'll understand things better."

They arrived. It went well, but the encounter in general was bizarre. I liked them, and missed them, but I hadn't felt intimate with them. I didn't know what to do.

"Oi! Are you not going to give your grandmother a kiss?"

"I still can't. I'm finishing the cleaning at present. At the moment, I still can't even hug people. You came from the street and passed by bars, cemeteries, together with so many other places with powerful energy. And I'm here, bathing in herbs on a daily basis. My body couldn't be cleaner. If I do come into contact with some form of negative energy, I'll probably pass out!"

"How grown up my granddaughter has become!"

I imagine that the reader, even a reader who doesn't believe any of this, must have at least a little curiosity about what Mãe Helena did with Turunga. I would be. What I can confirm is: what I went through was nothing like what you'd imagine. It was completely different to what you've heard Candomblé and Umbanda to be like.

I learnt some of the songs. That's probably the best way to put it, mantras! To pray and stabilise my energies. Anything else that is said is blasphemy, nonsense and slanderous.

When we are born, we awaken the primal energy that allows us to live in this world. We can call this mother-energy. Afro-Brazilian culture calls this energy Orisha. Orisha is an expression from Yoruba dialect and means: *Ori* = head; *xa* = earth; *Orisha* = head of the Earth.

This energy awakens us so that we are able to be born. This energy is pure and untainted. In our energy, there are both light and dark elements. The dark energies are channelled through our negative karmas. The light obviously passes through our positive ones, also known as dharmas. By teaching me about her culture and, in passing on her knowledge to me, Mãe Helena helped me to free myself from the dark elements that exist within my own energy.

I spent ten days in Mãe Helena's house, learning to make the special foods, teas and baths that I was going to need in the future.

When I returned home, I was an "*Iaô de Bessem*", an initiate. I was initiated by a nonconformist, by someone who had broken away from tradition. This was something that was to be repeated throughout my life.

# Mel

The car stopped at the porch of my aunt's house. I never lived with my parents in a house that they actually owned. By the time they were able to afford a property of their own, I was already an adult.

Well then, return home. This day affected me greatly. The first person that I saw was Edith's dead father.

I was different. Mãe Helena really did do something with me. She caused my first re-birth. I was 12 at this point. The two years prior to my meeting her had been horrific. I had suffered from sickness, had been unable to walk. I had had to tolerate Antenor, Edith's father, breathing constantly down my neck, every time I went into the street. He would retell me his story over and over again. He knew he was dead, but needed his daughter's forgiveness to be able to 'rest in peace'.

As I got closer to Antenor, I never again avoided conversation with the dead. I reckon that I would have been thoroughly traumatized, if I had been any older.

Mãe Helena totally disagreed when my father said to her I could be mentally ill. It wasn't just her. Every psychiatrist my father subsequently took me to, in his quest to prove that there was something mentally wrong with me, disagreed. He used to take me to be assessed by God only knows who. I'll always remember Mr Humberto attracting my father's attention, as my father came up with theories about the mental state of the people around him. That's right, about the people around him, rather than about his own!

I got out the car and looked at Antenor.

"Is he still here, sweetheart?"

"He is, mother. He can't hurt me with his negativity. Mãe Helena taught me how to protect myself against this; don't worry."

I mentally recited the mantras (let's stick with that as their name) and Antenor immediately began to distance himself. When this happened, straight away I began to trust Mãe Helena more.

My brothers were there on the tiled roof. This house didn't have a garden. Instead, on the patio, they had built a house for my parents to live in, but they never moved in. In fact, we ended up with the house on the roof, as the house below was constantly rented out to other families.

Anyone who has experienced a rebirth themselves will be able to relate, profoundly, to this story. It is a strange experience: incredible but strange nonetheless!

It was all the same: the buildings, the people; all exactly as they had been forty days prior... "Forty days?" I asked myself. "Yes, it had been only forty days", I muttered.

"What's wrong, sweetheart? Are you feeling ok?"

How is someone supposed to respond to that? I didn't. She repeated the question.

"Everything is the same, mum. Except me!"

"You've been through a lot, darling, but now everything is going to be ok. You're going back to school tomorrow. It has already been agreed with your teacher and with your headmistress. They both think you're intelligent and neither believe you will have any problems."

A brother, my aunt and Mezé came to see me.

"Turunga, you're different!" Maria José was the only one to notice.

"Mezé, can you do me a favour? Don't call me Turunga anymore; I don't want anyone to call me Turunga."

"So what are we going to call you then? Mercia is your mother's name and Celeste is your grandmother. Going with either of them will cause too much confusion. You call one; two reply! And the name Mercia Celeste is more popular than you'd care to realise..."

"Call me Mel, Mezé. That's what my schoolmates call me."

I was in grade seven. At school, no-one called me Turunga; they just called me Mercia. Suddenly, someone started to call me Mel.

To add weight to my decision, whenever someone referred to me as Turunga, I made the conscious choice not to respond to them. By doing this, people started referring to me as Mel at home too!

My life changed completely. I gave up playing with kites and marbles. Such childish games no longer appealed to me. Where Turunga had been talkative, open, happy, shy around people she didn't know and very active, Mel was old beyond her years, worldly-wise and wanted to work.

"So, where would you want to work? You're 12 years old. Who's going to give you a job?" my father asked.

I used to work in Arembepe and he never said anything about it.

"Arembepe was a small place at the beach. It's not the same here. You will have to catch the bus to work."

"Can I learn to walk to the bus?"

"Who's going to teach you?"

"I'll ask Mezé to take me out when she goes out. I'll learn that way."

"I suppose this may work."

I wasn't content with this. I wanted to do something grown up; to be grown up. I didn't like the routine at home. My father's family was depressing. They just didn't speak at home. My father spent his life shouting for silence and telling me and my younger brothers to shut up. It was a strange atmosphere and a mixture of fear, hate, frustration and unkindness were the norm in this house.

My mother used to go out. She said she couldn't take it, so would go to see friends, our cousins, aunts and uncles, but she never took us. There were too many of us to leave with other people to mind us. Besides, we had to go to school. By this point there were five of us; the youngest had already been born.

My father continued to study. He loved universities or other institutions of the like. He used to work at the *Banco do Estado* in the afternoons. The youngsters spent the days by themselves, with no one to watch over them but Mezé.

Then, one day, my father came up with an idea: we were going to sell shrimp. The restaurants and bars in Salvador preferred to buy from a middleman, instead of having to travel to the countryside, themselves. It wasn't worth it because of the quantity. So the middleman travelled, brought a tonne of shrimp and started to distribute it.

"A tonne, Milton? And where in God's name do you propose we keep these shrimp?"

"We'll store them here. I've already bought a large freezer. We'll sell them from here, too."

My mother tried to argue it, but eventually gave in. We had to give up our bedroom and ended up sleeping in the box room. Poor Mezé started sleeping in the kitchen. My father stayed in his bedroom, obviously! He had set up a 'business'. He would travel to Valença, a historic fishing town and it was there that he would buy the shrimp. The rest of the work was carried out by my mother, one of my brothers and me. My father's brother joined the business, but quickly left when he realised that it was an unachievable dream.

There was so much work involved and the house always stunk to high heaven of shrimp. We bought a car to help us with the deliveries to restaurants. My mother would do the deliveries and would take either me, or my brother, with her when she did. I didn't mind working, but working for my father meant that he was the only one who ever saw the profits we made. I personally delivered the orders made by his colleagues at the bank's branch he used to work at. Twenty or thirty kilos, every Friday, without fail. I delivered the steak of shrimp we prepared. God knows we stunk of shrimp.

Even my father eventually saw the futility of his little project. The whole neighbourhood started to complain about the fishy smell. They even went as far as threatening to take their complaint to the Ministry of Health and Sanitation, at which point my father gave in.

"Mum, I now know how to walk by myself to catch the bus and to the taxi rank. Can I get a job?" I asked.

"You're 13. Who's going to give you a job?"

In this past year, I saw Mãe Helena three times and, on my last visit, she made a point of saying:

"Your father doesn't want to bring you here anymore. The only reason you are still coming is because your mother put up such a fight for it."

"It's a damaged cause, Mãe Helena. He just doesn't want me to." I replied.

"I know, sweetheart. Pay attention and learn in silence. Do it for you. We are the only ones that know what is important in our own lives. Your father will try to pass on what he believes is important. Everyone does the same. It's rare to find someone who is capable of respecting other people's rights to make decisions. The things that I have taught you would be beneficial to everyone, including your parents, but we have to respect their decision not to."

"Would my father also need the herb baths, the chants and the recipes?"

"Yes, but he doesn't know this. He already has his own ideas about those who have a different coloured skin to him. In the past, he used to say that he didn't like these things and based his decision on gossip, intrigue, quackery and on the different things he had heard, which have nothing to do with what I have taught you. He's now given up this argument in favour of a new one: racial and social preconcept, because I'm so poor. I don't care, I don't respond; I don't have to defend myself. Those who feel the need to defend themselves do so because they are in the wrong and I'm not. Don't give up your studies. Your daily life revolves around it. You're going to grow up. You'll meet others who will be able to build upon the foundations I have given you. Don't cry, be strong. You're going to learn so much from this; in particular, how to be strong and not depend on anyone."

"Mãe Helena, I want to work, but my mother won't let me." I said, crying.

"I've already told you; don't cry; be strong. Believe in yourself and what you carry inside. What you have in your heart, and soul, is yours and there is nobody that can take it away from you."

"When we're at home he says that you are a follower of voodoo and that you sacrifice chickens."

"Let him say that. Let him spread his lies; it's ok. He only does this so that you tell him what I've taught you. Don't do it; don't tell him. Don't tell anyone."

"I know, Mãe Helena, otherwise I'll desecrate the knowledge!"

"Exactly, let him say what he wants. They're going to compare what I do to other spiritual practices. Let them do it; don't say anything!"

"Only open yourself up to those who are worthy. When you're older, you'll understand better. For now, let's go."

This was our final conversation. I only returned to see her after she died. It was the first time that I was happy to be able to see the spirits of those who had passed.

A year later, Mãe Helena passed away. I felt orphaned. I was only 14. I was working in a newsstand that my mother had bought to help pay the bills.

The newsstand was called *M. Ribeiro* and was located on Av. Joana Angelica, opposite the *ladeira da Independencia*. My brother and I helped my mother in this demanding new job. The newsstand used to open at 6am and would close at 11pm, almost every day. On Sundays, it would open at 7am and would then close at 9pm. We worked long hours to make ends meet. It got me out of the house, to the extent that I was never home. In the morning, I went to school. In the afternoons, and evenings, I was at the newsstand.

My grandmother passed away that same year. She was the only one who could ever control my father. This loss also affected me greatly. I cannot express how distraught I was and how much her death devastated me.

Her funeral was the first time that I had been to a cemetery.

"Mum, Mãe Helena used to say that it wasn't a good idea for me to go to cemeteries. I feel so very sad today and she taught me that such sadness weaken our energies."

"I know, darling, she told me the same thing. But if you don't go, your father will hit the roof. You know how he can be... let's not give him a reason to start."

When I entered the cemetery, I almost became lost in the crowd. Everywhere I looked, there were people who were still among the living. There were those who had passed away and every last one of them was wailing and in floods of tears. I covered my ears, breathed deeply and mentally recited the mantras Mãe Helena had taught me for times like this. Some spirits wanted to hold onto the arms and legs of the living; to get them to pay attention to them any way they could. Others just sat there, trying to talk to them. What nonsense.

"*Mel, here on the right, please.*"

This spirit was different to the others.

"How do you know my nickname?"

"*I'm a friend of the 'Breadman'. Do you remember him?*"

"He disappeared! Mãe Helena said that he would come back one day."

"*He didn't disappear. He just guided you from a distance. He didn't want to cause problems for you, given your family were unaware of your abilities.*"

"And you?"

"*Tommy! You can call me that, if you like. I'm here to help you. I'll be behind you, to your right. We won't lose contact. Don't be afraid; let's get you back to your family.*"

It was at this point that I realised how lost I was. I have no idea how I had made my way to the old 'wing' of the cemetery. Luckily, my new spirit friend took me back. His body gave off light, a gentle perfume and emitted a little cold. It was only afterwards that I learnt I felt cold because of the ether and what this meant.

Mentors are highly energetic, and organised, spirits and it is for this reason that they drive the fifth element towards the planet's material plane. The fifth element is the ether.

Mel didn't know any of this! All she knew was that she was lost, and afraid, in the cemetery.

"*Sweetheart! Hey you, girl! I know you see and hear me! Come here!*"

"*Ignore it, Mel; just keep going!*"

"Can I recite the mantras that Mãe Helena taught me?"

"*Of course! Go on.*"

My mother was beside herself when I reached her.

"Mércia Celeste, where were you? We've been looking everywhere for you. We even called you using the tannoy. The cemetery's security staff were looking for you, but they couldn't find you."

"I don't know what happened. I was walking. There was so much noise and so many people crying. I just got lost."

"Sweetheart, we've been looking for you for two hours!" my mother said, looking harassed.

"Are you sure?" Mel asked, sounding even more frightened.

Cemeteries are filled with powerful energies, that can confuse, and change, our sensory organs. Because of my hypersensitivity, I had attracted negative electromagnetic fluids; energy blocks that are common in hospitals, cemeteries, roads, hospices and prisons.

"Tommy, I want to throw up!"

"*You don't need to talk out loud to me. Think what you want to say. I'll hear you.*"

"That'd be better. If my father finds out that I've been talking to you, he'll lose it!"

"*Let's not cause you more problems, right Mel? You've grown up now and you're going to learn how to deal with your secrets like an adult.*"

"I learnt that keeping a secret isn't the same as lying. I'm gonna throw up."

I was so ill, to the point, they had to take me home.

"She was so fond of her grandmother. She's suffering so much, bless her!"

It was my aunt who said this, but I knew that the sickness had nothing to do with the pain of losing my grandmother. I was distraught. Not to the same extent the others were, but I already knew that I didn't view death the same way as the others.

At home, Tommy came to visit me.

"I'm feeling better in myself, yes. My head hurts though. Tommy, am I going to see my grandmother?"

"*Of course. But, for the time being, she's resting.*"

"Has she been able to find my grandfather?"

"Not yet, but she will. One day you'll understand all of this."

\* \* \*

A year later, I ran away from home. It was the second time that I had run away. The first was when I was 3 years old. When I ran away the second time, I hadn't quite turned 16.

Life at home was getting worse; not just mine, everyone's. My mother had decided that she wanted to take up studying about spirits and mediums. My father, naturally, disagreed, but she went ahead and did it anyway.

It was the first time that I had seen my mother successfully stand up to my father. She had often tried, but he always managed to make her back down. He used to fight with her and hit her until she backed down.

I felt so sorry for my mother. She worked with us in the newsstand and it was through this that my father's jealousy grew. My mother was beautiful, kind, friendly. To meet her was to like her.

Mel didn't understand how she had been able to go through with a marriage to such an unpleasant, angry man with so much baggage. One day he came to find my mother in the newsstand. We were working and my youngest sister was playing inside the newsstand. He had come to take her home.

"I can't, Milton! I'm not going to leave Mel here, on a Sunday, in this desert. It's dangerous."

"She's staying here, alright? It's not a problem. Mr Virgílio will be here later and he can stay with her. If you want, I'll call him now."

"No, Milton, it's not alright! He already owes the newsstand so much. If you start to ask him for favours then he'll feel that his debt has been repaid."

"You're trying to give me a morality lesson!"

"Go, mum; go with him. I'll stay here. I'll be ok."

"No, Mel! The match is about to end between Bahia and Vitória, the one where they're playing at Fonte Nova. It's going to be packed with people. I'm not leaving you here alone!"

"Right, I'm going to find her younger brother. He can stay with her." my father spat.

"He's at a friend's house. He went there to play." my mother hissed back.

"Why the hell did you allow that? Do you want to be here on your own; is that it? So that you can flirt!"

"I let him go because these children have no chance to play!

They are forever working. They go to school, come here, and then, from here, they go back to school!"

"Mum, go! I'll take care of the newsstand!"

"I'm not going, I've already said that! I'm going to stay and work. Who in God's name am I going to flirt with in the middle of the centre? Have you gone mad, Milton?"

My father lost it. He hit the car, driving it repeatedly into the newsstand whilst we were still inside. People had started to stop and stare, which resulted in him scurrying away feeling ashamed.

"Mum, go to Grandma Dulce's house. If you don't, he's going to start hitting you when you get home."

"Take your sister to the park to play. He's scaring her." my mother replied.

She was only 3 at the time and had become so frightened she had started to cry.

When my mother started to learn about spirituality, my father never cared much. Instead, he would just laugh at the books she would read:

"You fool! You left school before you learnt how to read properly." he would taunt her.

My mother just ignored him. She tried to set up a little study group with a friend. My father, naturally, disapproved but my mother was insistent. After a little while, a friend's husband decided to join them too. As you can imagine, my father didn't take kindly to this and started to make life hell for all concerned.

I used to enjoy spending time with them when they were studying, really so that I could learn more about mediumship and learn more about myself. The fight would start when we got home. My father wouldn't let any of us sleep. He would shout and, in his fit of rage, would beat my mother into next week.

My mother and I would go to work at 5am. We would open the newsstand at 6am and my father would be there sleeping. Sometimes my father wouldn't even go to work. He would spend the day sleeping and would then make up lies when he was next at work. It would start all over again in the evening. He was tired, as were we.

One day, my brother and I ran towards the door to call the police or get help from the neighbours. It was only when two officers turned up at the house that he stopped, although he soon found other ways to torture us. It was a difficult period.

Over time, I distanced myself from Mãe Helena's teaching. I stopped making the special dishes and stopped praying. I didn't have the time. I started to get sick again and my legs refused to walk. The tests, the hospital visits and the injections all started again.

"Milton, is she going to have to start all over again?"

"That woman, Helena, has already died hasn't she? What do you expect me to do?"

"We should look for Humberto and ask his help."

"He'll just say that it is all my fault, because I stopped the girl from seeing that woman. I don't want to hear this." my father retorted.

A month later, my mother went to find Humberto. I have no idea what they talked about. I was still in hospital and it was there that I met Pai Damásio. He took me out of the hospital, back to his home, where he cared for me.

I spent the next twenty days bathing in herbs, eating special dishes and praying. Pai Damásio was a strong man. He was black, but had bright brown eyes. He was in his 70's, but you wouldn't have thought it to look at him. Like Mãe Helena, he was one of those people who believe in the fundamentals of an idea but who doesn't agree with the way in which the idea, in this case of traditional Candomblé, is carried out and implemented.

"Helena prepared you well. It's a shame you stopped looking after your energies."

"You knew Mãe Helena? Did you belong to the same group? Were you friends? Did you spend much time together?"

"We were friends and agreed on most things."

"Did she ever mention me?"

"Oh yes, she mentioned you often! She knew that one day I was going to look after you. She left it to Humberto to see to that."

It had been so long since I felt truly happy; I was very important to her. She thought a lot of me. My father used to say, however, that she was only after the money.

"You have an open channel to the spirit world."

"What's that, Pai Damásio?"

"Between the physical world and the spirit world there is a portal made of energy. It's visible from the side closest to the corporal world, yet it is invisible to the side closest to the spirit world. There are people who can pass through this portal easily. They come and go as they please between the two worlds. You are one of these people."

"Are you one, too?"

"Me? No. I've studied these things but I have never seen or heard anything. Sometimes I feel a tingle down my spine and then someone's presence. Depending on the sensation, I am able to tell if the presence is at peace or not, like the spirits that haven't accepted death and who cling to this world, for example."

I knew about the spirits that haven't accepted death. I had read about them in the books written by Chico Xavier. Ten years after I first mentioned the 'Breadman', my mother decided to buy books to read through and she would give me some to read.

"You know I can see people who have died, as if they were still alive, don't you?"

"I do. Helena told me. This is good. The problem is that the energies in your house are disrupted, as a result of the presence of spirits who haven't accepted death. Your father doesn't look after his energies and he doesn't let anyone else in the house look after their own energies either. As a result, the people around him suffer, you more than most because you can see, hear and pass through the portal that the spirits, who cling to this world, use. One day, you will be able to go through the portal, to where there are only good spirits. When you arrive there, you will prove me right. You will see that your gift can be used for the greater good."

"When the time comes, I'll have grown up so will be able to make decisions for myself."

He smiled in agreement.

"You need to be careful. There are so many people out there who claim to know about these things yet who, in reality, just end up causing problems."

"How will I be able to tell the difference between the two types of people?"

"You'll know! You'll be able to tell from the energy they have around them. Your parents want to find someone who will make your abilities disappear. They asked me to be that person, but I told them that it's impossible. This is who you are. They are your reason for being. You'll eventually learn the reason you were born with these abilities. The problem you will find is that your parents may come across people who are dishonest. Be careful; don't go. If they make you; keep hush. You need only think of God and of the light."

When it happened, it was just like Pai Damásio had predicted, despite him having already taught me how to protect myself in situations such as these.

My father took me to a man in Valença. To this day, I have no idea how they knew each other. They probably met when my father was still selling shrimps. The man he took me to was beyond strange. He was skinny, but had a belly that stuck out slightly and was missing almost all his teeth. His breath stunk and his nails were long and filthy. As he walked, his body contorted and twisted with each step he took.

"Milton, how in God's name can you trust someone who looks like this?" my mother asked.

"What?! And you say I'm the judgemental one?"

"This has nothing to do with being judgemental, Milton. Not for a second do I believe that a person, who is clearly incapable of maintaining a decent standard of personal hygiene, is capable of teaching our daughter how to organise the energies around her."

"We're going to play it my way now. I've had enough of people like Humberto." he snarled.

He said he would work with me in the woods and that no-one would join us. We went somewhere where he kept plates made of clay and horrible black and red images made from plaster.

"Let's wait." he said to me.

I started to see spirits. They came in hoards, smiling and talking, grotesque expressions on their faces, swearing at each other. I felt fear creep up on me, but something incredible happened. I saw Mãe Helena appear and, in that instant, the fear subsided.

*"Get out of here. Go pray somewhere. Pray for forgiveness for your mistakes. Don't take your anger out on her."* She spoke in her usual, authoritative tone.

The man, who seemed to be waiting for God only knows what, chanted from one side to the other.

"Thank you, Mãe Helena." I called out silently.

*"It's ok, my angel. Be strong. Don't let on you saw me. I'm still here watching over you. Don't allow these things to scare you, not now, not ever. Have you forgotten what I taught you? Believe in what you have inside you; believe in your abilities. By doing this, you open yourself up to assistance and you won't need me anymore."*

She disappeared before I was able to ask her not to forsake me.

*"I will be here with you."* I heard her say, her voice resonating all around me.

"Let's get out of here. I don't know what happened. I think I got the wrong chicken. This one is old; it's weak. I needed a young one."

He opened the bag he had brought with us and the chicken jumped out.

"What are you going to do with this chicken?" I asked.

"I'm going to offer it as sacrifice to Zé Pelintra, so that he can prevent the spirits from coming near you again. Your father has already said this is all okay. One chicken a week should work, but I bought an old one. Do you think that this is why it didn't work?"

I stood there in silence. If only it had been possible to make myself deaf, so that I didn't have to listen to the man drone on until we had made it back to his home. I don't even remember his name, thank God.

"So? Did it all go ok?" my father asked the man.

"No, the person that was going to make it work didn't show up."

"Why not?"

"I don't know, Milton. I don't know if it was because the chicken was old, or because I charged you so little."

"Don't start your nonsense, mate. Now you're wanting to increase the price?"

"I'm being serious, Milton. Come back next week. I'm going to find out why it didn't work. I'll go to my Ialorixa's house and will ask her."

"Then we'll go today. I can't come back next week. We live in Salvador; you know this."

I looked at my mother and followed my father, and this random man, to his Ialorixa's house. But to do what?

It was a country house. In the doorway there were images similar to those I had seen in the woods. They were big, more than a metre in height. We went inside the house and were told to wait. As soon as I entered, I started to see the spirits again. I don't know if they were the same ones I had seen earlier, but they looked very similar.

"*Focus, don't let the fear take you.*" I heard Mãe Helena's voice in my head.

She spoke using telepathy. Time and space do not matter to good spirits as they are able to move at the speed of light.

Mel looked around for Mãe Helena, who simply repeated:

"*Focus, don't let the fear take you.*"

I took a few, deep breaths and repeated silently the mantras she had taught me, together with those that Pai Damásio had taught me. It worked. They didn't come near me.

When I opened my eyes, my mother was looking at me. I smiled at her. As they had said I would, I knew that I was in a place where the energy was powerful and I understood which side it belonged to.

"The Ialorixa is going to understand why I failed." the man from Valença said.

They agreed a price. My father complained about paying, saying that he shouldn't have to but, by this point, it was too late and money had exchanged hands. The person that we ended up meeting was a woman, dressed in a red skirt, a pink blouse, bracelets and bangles. She summoned the spirit that helped her in her work. She spoke loudly, her voice booming as she roared, all the time drinking whiskey and cider.

I focused on my mantras and, once again, I heard Mãe Helena's voice.

"*This is a spirit of such enormity and it is unable to help anyone. Stay calm. This spirit will show you respect. It already knows it has no hold over you.*"

"You're wasting your time." the spirit said to my father.

"You can give him the money back; there's no point in continuing. The girl has come here with someone watching over her. She belongs to the light and to the realm on high. I don't want to make problems for myself. I only work with people who are worse than I am. This girl has never hurt anyone. It's a waste of time."

"They told me that you were able to solve anything! That's why I don't believe any of this."

"Believe what you like. It appears you don't want your daughter, or your wife, to be a part of this. The disturbances around you don't allow you to believe, simply for the fact they enjoy seeing the fights. The energy in your house is disrupted, as is yours, but I don't want to cause problems for myself. Give him back his money and send him on his way. I'm trying to do you a favour by making sure you don't come into contact with people who are worse than me. Leave; get out! Get the girl out of here before she weakens the energies in my house!"

We left quickly, got back into the car and drove straight back to Salvador. We didn't eat anything that day. My father didn't say a word to me in the car. He only started to talk when we got home:

"Do they make this up as they go along?"

"Milton, Mãe Helena and Pai Damásio have helped our daughter. You can't deny that."

"They helped because they wanted someone white in their homes, to boost the number of clients they have."

"Father, don't say that. You know it's not true!"

"Shut your mouth! You want the back of my hand? Get the hell out of our lives! You've screwed everything up for us! You aren't wanted here!"

After he said that, instead of going to school, the next chance I got I ran away.

# Macarrão in São Paulo

"Today, Jair, I'm gonna catch the bus in Ibotirama. There are no age restrictions for passengers who wish to buy tickets and travel by themselves, even to São Paulo."

"Are you sure, Macarrão?"

"Yes, Jair. I can't carry on like this. I can't keep fleeing, running here and there. It's been almost a year since I ran away. I need to work out where my life is going. Thank you for everything. After my grandparents, Mãe Helena and Pai Damásio, you've been my best friend. You've been like a father to me, like the real father I never had."

"So you're going to São Paulo, Macarrão? It's not often I go there. Stay here, in Bahia, in Ibotirama itself. No-one's going to find you."

"It's São Paulo, Jair. That's where fate is calling me."

"Did your spirit friend tell you that?"

"Not as such; I just dreamt that I had to go to São Paulo. The spirits don't send anything like that my way; they have no reason to."

"I know, I know, but what is their take on it all?"

"I haven't asked. When I told my friend about the dream, he just fell about laughing. It's difficult to explain why they are the way they are."

"It's ok, Macarrão; just make sure you keep in touch."

A tight hug, a few tears and a handshake. That was how we would say goodbye. His eyes had welled up to the point they clearly stung. My eyes, on the other hand, sparkled with hope.

In Ibotirama, he bought me a rucksack, a pair of jeans, a few tops and a pair of trainers. We said goodbye at the entrance to the city where I was due to catch the bus.

The truth is that the chapter of my life that had Jair in it started with me hitch-hiking. When we met, I was afraid to tell him that I was running away from home. I tried so hard to come up with a lie that I thought he would believe. We were both on the ferryboat leaving Salvador and heading to Itaparica, when I asked him for a ride.

"I live inland. My mother is sick; I'm on my way to see her!"

"Why are you wearing a uniform?" he asked, looking at my clothes.

"I heard the news about my mother when I was at school, but I don't have enough money to get a bus ticket."

"I'm on my way to *Bom Jesus da Lapa*. What about you?"

"I'm not going far." I didn't know what to say.

"Be my guest!"

I remember thanking God that he hadn't pushed for an answer. When we reached land, we found some pilgrims. The journey was going to take a while and conditions were harsh. I had always wanted to go on a pilgrimage. I loved the idea of them. Things were off to a good start, I thought.

If you've never been on a pilgrimage, it's one of those things that you need to take part in to understand what faith and belief are. You have to be part of it from the start, as I was. You have to travel in the lorries, sitting on wooden benches, undergoing all conditions.

My journey lasted two whole days. The rain was torrential for most of it, to the point we even had to stop. I was travelling in the front with Jair. In the back, there were twelve adults and four children sat in rows. They were eating the toasted manioc flour that they had kept in empty tins that had once contained powdered milk. The women were dressed in white and wore hats with red ribbons. The men wore white trousers and shirts. In the end, their white clothes never lasted, due to the dusty roads.

I had never before seen such faith. They were sat there, without any back support, for two days as we travelled, all huddled, at the base of the lorry. Some people had come further than me; some even from other states. Some had even been travelling for a week in these conditions.

*Into the horizon, step by step I journey forth,*
*Along this path of light that guides me home,*
*I am a pilgrim from lands afar,*
*A pilgrim with heart and soul.*

They sang and prayed. It was such a profound thing to witness. Just being around these people was enough to plant the seeds of faith and I too found myself beginning to sing along.

"Do you plan on becoming a pilgrim?" Jair asked.

"Can I? Would you let me?"

"Ah! So you aren't going to see your sick mother? Wasn't that what you told me yesterday?"

"Yes, it was, but it wasn't true."

"I'm confused!"

"Listen, it's like this. My father beats me and he threw me out... because I see the spirits of those who have passed away, as if they were still alive. I'm a medium and I need to protect my psychic energies. He wants me to stop seeing them, but it's not that simple."

"Listen, I may be a Catholic but I'm also a spiritualist. My mother had the ability to call the spirit of an Indian woman into herself and used to give out herbal remedies to the poor. She managed to cure many of the people who lived in our area. What you're saying about yourself; is it all true?"

I told him everything I could. He listened to what I had to say, looking intently at me the whole time, before diverting his gaze to the road.

"How old are you?"

"Going on 16!"

"You look younger, but when you talk... you seem wise beyond your years. Look, I believe you. You can stay with us but, if I catch you doing something you shouldn't, I'll have to give you over to the police."

"So, what constitutes 'doing something I shouldn't'?"

"Smoking, drugs, drinking or having indiscretions. I don't believe these to be appropriate."

"I don't like such things either! Not only do I not like them, I'd be afraid to try these things. That's why I asked you if I could hitch-hike with you."

"What do you mean?"

"Well, you're old and old people don't like the things you said."

"You think I'm old?"

"Well, yeah. I think you're old, but you have a nice face and you look like the organised type. I can tell these things. Pai Damásio taught me well."

"What's your actual name, my little white angel?"

"Mercia Celeste."

"I'm gonna call you Macarrão, because you're really skinny. You remind me of the long, thin pieces of pasta from back home. Talking of which, we're gonna stop soon. I'm so damned hungry."

"Should I stay here, Jair?"

"Yes! You're teaching your parents a lesson they won't forget. We can decide later what to do!"

During the pilgrimage, we stayed in *Bom Jesus da Lapa* and our friendship blossomed.

Jair proved himself to be a good man. Whenever we saw a police car, he would make a point of hiding me from sight, on the off chance that my parents had alerted the police to my disappearance.

I managed to convince Jair that I shouldn't return home. I was able to convince him I shouldn't because I believed it so wholeheartedly. I didn't want to go back only to have more problems with my family. I used to imagine that, with me gone, the fights would subside. At least, I found it comforting to think like this. Something told me that leaving home had, in fact, been my destiny.

We spent a week in *Bom Jesus da Lapa*. At the end of the week, Jair received an order of onions, which we then proceeded to deliver together.

A month later, and God only knows how or why, my parents turned up in *Bom Jesus da Lapa* - some 500 miles away from Salvador. I guess they were just following leads. Someone would see something and tell the police who would, in turn, tell my parents. At this point, though, I was long gone, following my destiny into the sunset.

Macarrão didn't know anything about apprenticeships, spiritual journeys, detachment, self-confidence or independence. I continued to pray and chant my mantras. It seemed logical. Everything made sense. Not even Halu Gamashi knows how Mel became Macarrão. How did she manage to pluck up courage to set out on this journey?

Over time, Macarrão travelled every inch of Brazil. On her travels, she met some of the most weird and wonderful people you could wish to meet; she ate foods you'll never have even dreamt existed; she swam in rivers and seas that are worlds apart from one another and allowed her faith to flourish and develop. She found a Bible in the glove box of the lorry they were travelling in. Throughout the journey, she read it from cover to cover and discussed every aspect of it with Jair.

As they travelled across Brazil, Macarrão saw the different types, and degrees, of Catholicism. She already knew what the Catholics back home were like, how superstitious they were and how these superstitions derived from African culture. She learnt about indigenous Catholics, where *Tupã* replaced Jesus and the Holy Virgin competed with *Yara* for the people's faith.

This is how Macarrão's life was, until the day came when she had to say goodbye and flee to São Paulo.

# Arrival in São Paulo

"Upon my steed; I set your soul free, Prometheus."

"Shut up, you fool!"

"We don't have to listen to this music! There's a few of us here! You need to learn to respect other people's opinion!"

"Shut up, you fool!"

Mel woke up in the middle of this 'slanging match'. She was on a bus, half filled with locals and half with construction workers, in the Sertão of Bahia.

The reason the slanging match had started was because one of the boys in the group was insistent on singing protest music. Mel got up and walked over to the boy:

"Oi, kid; you got people here trying to sleep. Keep the noise down."

"Who are you?"

"I've come to stop you getting a beating."

"Sit there, let's talk."

"What's your name?"

Intuitively, Mel knew that she could trust this boy. His name was Adonias. He had run away from the starvation, and the lack of resources, in the Sertão of Bahia five years ago. Since then, he had been living on the outskirts of São Paulo and was studying psychology in Mogi das Cruzes.

"When I arrived in São Paulo, I started working in construction. I used to carry bags of cement on my head and would have bags of gravel strapped to my back. It was a hard life. They nicknamed me 'Bahia Boy', as if this was in any way a nickname. They would all laugh whenever I said anything, because of my accent. They put stuff in my food, but everything was ok. I transcended. I took courses aimed at adults and also became a Buddhist."

"A Buddhist, Adonias?"

"You can call me Bida. And yes, I became a Buddhist; firstly, because of the food - it was free. They would give me food every day and I used to enjoy the dances. The smell of the incense reminded me of the Sertão, when it used to rain. I would read their books and was drawn into their way of life. I fell for a girl who studied psychology and decided that I was going to study it too. I got a job, and later managed to retire as mentally ill.

"What the hell? Tell me everything."

Bida explained everything. He told Mel a long story about how this girl encouraged him to retire with a fake ill-health diagnosis.

"I gave up on everything. I stopped shaving; stopped bathing. I stumbled across a little place where there were bees and hornets and ended up having to go to the doctor. They'd attacked every inch of my body. This was the only way for me to study at the university. When I graduate, I'm going to do all I can to set everything right."

The bus stopped.

"Should we get something to eat? We can share..."

Mel thought it odd this specific invite to share 'a meal'.

Bida explained:

"I make this journey twice each year and I already know this stop. There really is so much food."

During the journey, Mel and Bida became friends. She continued the journey next to him, listening and laughing along to his stories. He was what might be considered stereotypically as a *Sertanejo*; someone who had left the hard life in the Sertão and made his way to São Paulo to work in the construction industry. Once there, he became a Buddhist, a psychology student and was engaged to a psychologist. He was the ideal person to teach Mel about São Paulo, as well as how cruel life can be, and those moments of madness that we need to experience to be able to jump through the impossible hoops life brings our way.

When she arrived in São Paulo, Mel followed Bida back to his home. She had arrived in São Paulo in the winter. She knew nothing of São Paulo, or of its fluctuating temperatures. That was the night that this drop in temperature hit them. The houses were not built for this, as they lacked hot water in sinks and heaters. Fear began to set in; both about the temperature and also her first trip on the metro. She had heard of a nearby metro station, called the *Estação da luz* (Station of Light). For Mel, however, when she thought of a 'Station of Light', she thought of the Eiffel Tower, lit up against the black sky, surrounded by a thousand Christmas trees shining like stars in the night.

The *Estação da Luz* in São Paulo acted like a big house. It was partially square, partially in darkness, with a seemingly endless number of people sleeping on the floor, their faces hidden as best as possible to protect against the bitter cold. All around, noises from the passing trains could be heard, which were then echoed by sounds of panic and fear.

"Mel, there! We're going to run; that's our train! It's only an hour from here to Poá. What did you think of the *Estação da Luz*?"

She thought about asking Bida why he indulged her fantasies. On the bus, for as long as they were travelling, Mel told him exactly what she had expected from the *Estação da Luz*. Bida sat in silence listening, as though he agreed with the scene she was innocently describing for him. Mel thought about picking a fight with him:

"Were you laughing at me when you told me about the *Estação da Luz*?"

She decided against it. It was better like this. He had said that they needed to run. This was true. The first thing she learnt in São Paulo was that you have to run. You don't have the luxury to disappear into your own little world; you just have to run... to seize the day.

Poá was bathed in shadow. It was cold. It was silent. It never occurred to Mel that, at the time she was there, she was only 16 years old. She was wondering the streets of a strange city with a complete stranger. All she knew was that she was with Bida – psychology student, Buddhist and good friend. She hadn't even spent two whole days with him, yet she already considered him a good friend. But did he feel the same way?

"Mother, Raquel, Zé Carlos, this is Mel. I met her on the bus. She seems nice. She's coming to live in São Paulo. Out of interest, why is it that you are coming to live here?"

This is how she was introduced to Bida's family. She didn't respond to the question. They didn't give her chance.

There, between the introductions and the greetings, Mel understood Bida had spent three months away from São Paulo. He had gone to bury his son who had passed away. He was only 8, bless his soul, born to a woman called Maria in the Sertão. They didn't talk much, so Mel didn't register her full name.

The boy had died from unknown causes. His name had been Prometheus.

"I had read the legend and liked the name, so I gave him it as his name. I also made him a promise: when I qualify, I'll open a centre to teach about Buddhist culture in the Sertão. Now that he's gone, I don't know if I want to go through with the promise."

"So that's why you were singing a song that had the name Prometheus in it, when we were on the bus?"

"Mel, I want you to promise me that you won't let this city make you bitter. Promise me that you won't let it drive you mad."

Mel learnt from Bida that sometimes it is necessary to go slightly mad, in order to not lose yourself completely. A type of madness with a pinch of lucidity; when you let your hair down, so that you have the strength to make it through challenges life throws at you. The cruelty that's hidden in life's challenges, when pitted against one's sanity, can be enough to drive you eternally mad.

Mel struggled to find her feet in São Paulo. She learnt about Buddhism with Bida and the day-to-day fight the working class had to endure to survive.

"Bida, I think Buddhism is like Candomblé, which I learnt from Mãe Helena and from Pai Damásio. It involves singing, dancing, food offerings to the Almighty and eating holy food. This feeling of brotherhood where everyone is equal."

"Bida, this is the second time that I have seen Lula. The first time was in Joana Angelica, a street in Salvador. He was walking shouting: "The people are not afraid, down with Figueiredo".

"Bida, what does a psychologist do?"

Bida was Mel's friend. He helped her get a job as a market researcher. In the evenings, she would go with him to the university in Mogi das Cruzes. Mel sold working class journals to lecturers and administration staff in the university, whilst Bida attended the classes.

"If someone, who looks square, comes here with a grimace on their face, you need to stick the journals under your arm and act like you're one of the students."

"Bida, how do you look square?"

"You know, people who looks like they aren't getting any and who have a face like a slapped arse because of it. I don't know how else to explain it to you; you'll have to make do with that."

"Bida, just one more thing: how am I supposed to pass myself off as a student?"

"Act like a hippy. Walk with your legs apart, chew your pen lid and look like you know a lot about a lot of things."

Through doing this Mel learnt, not only about other people and their behaviour, but also about herself. She sympathised with Buddhism and rebelled, in favour of the working classes. She read journals so that she could talk about them to the people she was selling them to. She took up smoking, like the Europeans, without a filter. Smoking with a filter was something that the bourgeoisie did. She didn't smoke pot, as she didn't like the smell.

"It's for the best that you don't like pot; you're already distant. You have a head filled with imagination and an unparalleled awareness. Stay away from drugs, Mel. You don't need them, nor they you."

"What about beer?"

This is how Mel started drinking beer and smoking unfiltered cigarettes. She also took part in a strike at the university and was forced to flee from the police, and their dogs, and from moral bombs. Mel had never felt more alive. She had found a reason to fight; a cause to defend.

She signed up as a volunteer for different works that were carried out in the slums and became familiar with the world of drug trafficking.

"Bida, traffickers are people who traffic drugs. Lobbyists are people who spread poisonous ideas. What about the people?"

He never replied to these questions.

Bida liked Mel. One day, she surprised him as he was talking about her to a friend:

"She's a good kid. When I first met her, I thought her half mad. She came here talking about seeing the dead, as though they were still alive. I thought her nuts."

"So, isn't she?"

"No, she's not, Edson. She saw my father stood by my mother's side. She described him perfectly… even down to the way he used to talk. I was impressed, but there's more. She also saw, described and passed on a message from my girlfriend's brother."

"Do these seers not live in the Spirit Centre, then? My mother has a friend who is a medium and her and Mel are polar opposites. She doesn't drink, or smoke. She's been completely caught up in the system. Mel is different. She's revolutionary; she tells jokes and dances…"

"Exactly, she does all those things. The only thing that strikes me as odd is that she doesn't talk about her family at all. She ran away from home; she doesn't talk about life back home; she never gives any indication about what happened in her past."

Mel thought about going into the room and saying to Bida that there was nothing to talk about, but thought better of it. Her life was what she was now living. Here she felt useful. What would he say? She didn't know. She missed her brothers, her mother and even, at times, her father… she missed them all.

Mel, however, questioned her feelings. Turunga never used to. Mel grew and, until this day, Halu Gamashi has been unable to solve this: she doesn't know how to talk about her feelings. Even writing about it is difficult.

Love, for me, is a strong and silent feeling. To love is to wholeheartedly give yourself and trust someone. Without this trust, love cannot exist. This is what I believe.

I was an odd child… I was different. I was a conflicted adolescent. My family could never understand my turmoil. My relatives thought me half mad. My brothers considered me a burden.

"Mel, forget this 'nonsense' about seeing spirits. You know that anyone who knows father stops playing these games early on. Life is hard enough already and there you are trying to make it harder." one of my brothers told me.

What should I say to Bida now?

Mel was accepted. She didn't bring problems with her and believed she had found a family who liked her.

# Mel: The art of stealing

"Pay attention to the plan, Mel. You're going to go into the market. Grab a basket. Only put food in it. Do you understand? Only get food; beans, rice, fish, salt… you know…. food. Go to the checkout, like you're getting ready to pay. Normally, there'll be a queue. I want you to join this. I'll be waiting at the entrance to the market. When it's your turn to pay, put the basket on the checkout. I'll burst in, snatch the basket from you, push you and I want you to pretend to fall to the floor. I'll run out, whilst you lie there on the ground. Act scared, shaken up, like it's not your fault, ok?"

"I don't know, Bida. Will it work?"

"Of course! The market owner is an exploiter. Have you not seen the prices? Every day they are higher than they were just 24 hours before. He's bourgeois. Have you seen his car? It's so fancy…

Bida talked and talked. We didn't just steal for the sake of stealing, though. José Carlos, Bida's brother, was unemployed and had been for the past three months. Raquel didn't work either; rather she stayed home to care for their sick mother.

After I arrived from Bahia with Bida, three more of his relatives arrived: a brother, his wife and their child. There were eight of us in the house and Bida was only on a minimum wage.

The money I made from completing the market research was never guaranteed and what I earned from selling the paper brought in a pittance. I was a minor in the eyes of the law, being only 16.

In all honesty, the reason we stole was because, otherwise, we would have gone hungry. It had already been two days since we last ate. The last thing we actually ate was a soup made from unripened bananas which had, incidentally, also been stolen by José Carols from the far end of the house. What else were we to do?

"Come on, Mel. You have to join in. You're part of the family now. You're white, well presented and have an honest face. No-one will be able to not trust you."

"What would Buddha say about this?" I tried to make him see reason.

"Dunno. If I bump into him one day, I'll ask him. If he doesn't approve, knock him into next week. So tell me, you gonna go or not? We're all hungry."

"Alright. It's God's will." I said, not really believing my own words.

We went over the plan from start to finish and it went almost exactly as we had hoped but... I forgot to fall to the floor. I forgot to appear shaken up, which I'll put down to genuine nerves. The checkout girl looked at me and recognised me. She had seen me with Bida, either on the train or around the place.

"They're friends! I know those two!"

"Is this true, girl?" the security guard asked, clenching my fist.

"It is, it is true, sir."

They called the owner of the market and took me to his office.

"Well, girl. What do you have to say for yourself?"

The owner of the market was a young man and was friendly. He was so calm. His posture made me more at ease. He gave me the chance to talk, so I explained. If he had shouted, or thrown accusations around, I wouldn't have said anything. I don't know how to defend myself. If someone says something to upset me, I just ignore them and let them carry on thinking whatever it is they want to think. I don't know any different. On this occasion, however, it wasn't necessary. Alceu, the owner of the market, spoke calmly whilst the security guard screamed about how he was going to call the police and beat me.

"Shut up, man! Let the girl talk!"

"If you want, Mr Alceu, I'll take you to where I live, then you'll see without me having to explain. You'll see what it's like."

"You can explain, child; I'll believe you."

I told him about our hunger, about the paper. I didn't tell him anything about Bida's work though. I thought it better that way. What would I have said?

"Mr Alceu, it was wrong of me to do what I did. I know that. I didn't even want to do what I did."

"Why didn't you run? The security guard was nowhere near you. That's actually the reason I'm hearing your side. I saw it all; you could have run with your friend. So why didn't you?"

"I didn't have the strength to, Mr Alceu. I was so nervous." I almost let slip that I was already on the run; that I had run away from Bahia and from my family. Mr Alceu didn't give me the chance.

"Make a list of what you took."

I made a list and handed it to him.

"I'll think of this as a loan. Pay me back when you can. I'll set up a tab here for you to use whenever you want, or need, to. All I ask is that you don't do this again. If you do, next time you won't be as nervous. If you carry on doing what you're doing, you'll become a thief. As time goes by, you'll become cold and bitter and, the saddest thing is, you won't even see the change. It'll change you completely. Is this what you want?"

"No, Mr Alceu. I really don't want to be like that!"

"Then it's sorted. You can go. Tell your friend to use better judgement in the future."

At home, everyone was eating.

"Mel, come eat something. Tell me what happened."

Even though I was hungry, I couldn't bring myself to eat. I told Bida about my conversation with Alceu.

"You shouldn't believe everything he said; you're young. He wasn't going to get anything if he had you detained. Bloody bourgeoisie! Don't believe what he told you."

"Bida, I think you're becoming cold-hearted. What was it you told me when I came here? 'Mel, I want you to promise me that you won't let this city make you cold-hearted and bitter.'"

He looked me in the eye and said:

"I need to help my family and I want to graduate from Uni.

I'll think about other things afterwards."

"Well then, Bida. Maybe it's too late."

We didn't talk about this again. I paid back what I owed. I ran errands for Alceu and the slate was wiped clean.

This episode drove a wedge between Mel and Bida. I don't know why. Even they didn't know why, but it did. Mel stopped going to the university to sell books. Bida stopped playing taxi.

"I changed group. The people there, they talk and talk but that's all it is."

"How come, Bida?"

"They talk and write articles. They reject it without proof, but it doesn't amount to anything. I'm now with another group. It's rough. It's better you stay clear of this. You're still a baby."

The divide grew between them. Mel started walking by herself again. She spent the whole day doing research. A work colleague introduced Mel to another company and the research doubled. She now worked during the day and, at times, through the night, just to make ends meet. The money improved.

One day, Bida came home as the sun was coming up.

"Mel, Mel, wake up!"

"What's wrong, Bida?"

"Have you got any money?"

"No, I don't get paid until the end of the week. I did the shopping with what I had. Why do you ask?"

"No reason."

Bida was acting odd; he always seemed nervous.

So the time came for Mel to leave. She sorted her backpack, said goodbye to everyone and went on her way.

She went on her way. Whatever path that was. It is difficult to write about this.

Ever since I was a child, there has always been a force in me, guiding me. It guides me alongside my conscience. It's a voice I hear; a guiding light that shows me logic and which path to follow. Then, off I go. I follow this inner certainty. As I said, it's difficult for me to talk about it, to explain it to other people.

I possess an unspoken certainty. It's not a rationale per se, but a vast amount of knowledge. So there I go. I follow this certainty.

It's stronger than I am. Then suddenly, the voice, the certainty takes over and I... I obey. I obey because I know it to be the correct thing, the done thing to do.

When it comes, it tells me: "Now is the time to leave. Your time here has come to an end."

So there I went, without ever looking back. It was this that made it easier to run away from home. I know that it may come across as insanity, but that doesn't make it any less true.

* * *

Whilst we are talking about the truth, I want to take a moment to express how difficult it is to write about oneself. What to say? What stories should I tell? It's time to talk a bit about this.

This is the way I write: fluently. I hope that the past, and present, merge and join in my writings.

Now is the time to talk about my selection criteria. What did I base my decisions on with regards to the stories to tell and the people to mention when writing this book?

*Chakras: The True Story of a Medium* is a book that has changed me greatly. I only decided to write it because my life made it necessary. At the start of the book, in the introduction, I explained my reasons. There were people who found out about me and about the spiritual experiences I have.

I was approached by many people. Some wanted to turn me into the new Chico Xavier, the most famous, spiritual medium in Brazil. He was a good, very enlightened man who shed light, for the Brazilian people, on the science behind mediumship although, in my opinion, very few people actually understood his work.

People generally look for gurus who can help them with their problems. If these gurus are able to provide people with the help they need, at the time they need it, then they are rewarded with names such as: 'Enlightened; Master; Christ; Buddha'. If they don't achieve what they hoped, then the names the guru will be branded with are contrary to the above cited names. I have experienced this throughout my own life.

I have also come across people who wanted to initiate protests and demonstrations. I didn't; that wasn't my aim.

Then there were those who were attracted to the money, and fame, that comes with the territory of being a well-known medium. There the voice changes, and the voice that tells me when it's time to leave appears. It's happened all throughout my life. I've known different people and have played a part in their stories and their lives.

The stories I have chosen to write out aim to highlight how I have come to be where I am now. I have chosen moments in my life that have helped mould my character, my shadow, my light, the spiritual part of me and the light in me that needs to be shaped. By living through Turunga, Mel, Mercinha and Halu Gamashi, the paths down which I have journeyed are many. In the selection process, I filtered out stories I wanted to tell by using only those that didn't reduce me to tears when I remembered them and by picking those that didn't make me think any more, or less, of the people they involve. Naturally, there were other criteria but, in all honesty, this was the main one.

Right, you're going to have to wait until the end of the book before you fully know me. If that isn't good enough, come and find me. If you're interested in finding out how a paranormal lives day-to-day, or you want to learn how my chakras opened and live real, spiritual experiences, then I would make a great companion.

I have been given many offers over the course of my life. Some of them I accepted; others I didn't. Some of my choices were good; others were not. It is important to be able to choose, to learn how to live with your mistakes and grow as a person. This is the philosophy by which I live my life: learn from experience. I respect all other theoretical philosophies and use them as a source of inspiration. I don't, however, believe in theoretical, or imaginative, growing.

One of the proposals I received, and which I refused, was to have someone else write this book about me.

A famous author, interested in my story, had been scouted but I wasn't interested. Back then, I didn't go for it because I wasn't ready to expose myself. However, I always knew that, when the time came for me to expose my secrets to the world, it would have to be me, myself, to give them up just as I am doing now.

Telling people stories can be such a minefield and, telling certain stories, is like many minefields joined together. There are always two sides to any story and every story can be interpreted in different ways. For this reason, I don't know how stories are told... no-one does. The ways in which they can be told can only be counted. I'm not a number; there isn't just one truth to me. Nobody is a number; there isn't just one truth to anyone. When we tell a story, the closest we can get to the truth is our own, personal interpretation of the facts.

When I tell this story, I look at the way I lived, and felt, under the weight of being different in a world where everyone strives to be the same.

Belonging to a minority is not easy. I belong to a minority or, rather, I belong to a group of minorities. The smallest of these minorities is a group of people who are from here, there and everywhere, who have no interest in being slaves, or masters, or being any better, or worse, than anyone else. In my opinion, this is the hardest minority to be in, out of all those I identify with.

But Mel didn't know about minorities. I'll leave Halu Gamashi here with her pains, her loves and her memories. I'll go back to embodying the rebel, Mel.

Was Mel sweet? I don't remember. This nickname was born from a variant of the name, Mércia. So was Mércia sweet? I don't know anything about her. I never co-existed with her.

Mércia Celeste Dias da Silva is the headline of my life story. It tells the story of Turunga, Macarrão, Mel and Halu Gamashi.

The part of me that belongs to Halu Gamashi is strong! It's difficult to walk away, however... it helps me understand that memories are like flowers in spring: they sprout; they grow; they blossom.

Whilst I allow Mel to take me over, Halu Gamashi still shines through in my emotion. Both parts channel through me together, almost touching.

The Mel part of me is a rebel: innocent; feisty. She has a petite body, dresses in jeans and t-shirt and a piece of string tied around her wrist. The Halu Gamashi part of me is heavier and covered in scars.

In the centre of Halu Gamashi's forehead, there is a white mark. It's vertical and marks the spot where her frontal chakra repeatedly opened. In the centre of her palms there are two round scars and, on the backs of her hands, there are three circles, each having appeared when the upper synesthetic chakras opened. On her chest there is a deep round mark, which shows where her heart chakra opened repeatedly. On her chest there is also another scar. This one is short and appeared following the cardiac surgery that was undertaken when she suffered from rheumatic fever.

On her abdomen there is a vertical trail to show where her solar plexus chakra opened. This chakra, however, only opened once. In the centre of her knees there is a circle where the Kundalini chakras opened and, in the middle of her feet, two circles where the lower synesthetic chakras opened.

When the upper chakras opened, Halu Gamashi became acquainted with the Astral Houses, the place to which we all go when we slumber, where there is higher spirituality, light, honour and glory; the immortal place to which we are all destined to go one day, when we finally win the battle with spirits clinging to what once was and the shadows that accompany them; shadows about which Halu Gamashi developed knowledge when the lower chakras opened.

I sometimes think about Mel, carrying all her bags, not long after she had ceased living with Bida, when she was looking for a new place to live.

"Oi girl, you come from Bahia, right?"

Mel looked around to see who was speaking and if the person was talking to her. The woman who had spoken to her was black and was dressed completely in white, with a turban on her head. Mel stopped to speak to her.

"What part of Bahia are you from?"

"I'm from Jequié. When I was 3, we went to live in Santo Amaro da Purificação. At the age of 6, we then moved to Salvador. I stayed there for about 15 years." Mel replied anxiously.

"Where are you going now?"

"I'm looking for somewhere to live."

"Well then, you're in luck. Come in; I'm the owner of an Umbanda Centre. We can set up a society. All you need to do is tell people you are from Bahia, nothing more. I'll take care of the rest."

Mel couldn't understand what the woman was talking about, but she followed her in silence. She was looking for somewhere to live, after all.

"This is my Umbanda Centre. I have many clients, all of whom have a soft spot for people who come from Bahia. What's more, instead of just giving you a place to live, I can offer you work also, if you want? If my Parish grows because of your help, I'll give you some of the profits."

"What's your name?"

"Maria Antônia, but people know me as Maria da Luz. Being 'of the light' seems more fitting in my line of work."

Mel decided to simply call her Maria.

"Maria, I don't know anything about Umbanda. I'm only 16; who would believe a word I say? Besides, I don't have anything to say about the type of work you are suggesting."

"You don't get it, do you?"

"No, I don't, Maria."

"Come with me; you're going to live here in the Centre. Given time, you'll get to better understand what I'm saying and the type of work we do here. Do you have somewhere else to go? I know you don't. Are you willing to sleep in the cold? Do you have money? I've been watching you for some time now, living with Bida, and I am aware of the difficulties you have."

Maria asked questions, which she then answered herself, whilst Mel asked herself: "I don't have money to travel elsewhere, nor do I have anywhere to actually go. Should I, or should I not, accept this offer?"

She didn't accept the offer, nor did she turn it down.

"Maria, it would be good for me to sleep here if you were happy for me to do so, but we need to make something clear; I don't know anything about Umbanda. My work involves market research and studies."

"What's that?"

"A company launches a product and wants to know what

consumers think of it. So, what they do is hire someone who has experience in conducting research. This is what I do. I interview people in the street and go door-to-door."

"So, you meet a lot of people. I can make little business cards with my address, giving some information about my work, and you could hand them out. We can talk more about this later. Come on, I'll show you where you're going to be sleeping."

My country has many religions and an uncountable number of cultures. For a long time, Spanish and Portuguese thinking dominated, and determined, what Brazil's religion was going to be. From 1960 onwards, African religion, and culture, were common in Brazil's high society.

Anthropologists, artists and great thinkers infiltrated Afro-Brazilian religion and took it unto themselves to raise awareness about it through both Brazil and the rest of the world. Attracted by the diverse ways of thinking, the legends, singing, poetry and fashions, they found Afro-Brazilian religion to be a fertile breeding ground for their own beliefs and aspirations.

On the other hand, this religious sect culture needed icons, which were respected by cultural and fashion-driven society when spreading the word about them, in an attempt to attract followers. Popularity grew. Afro-Brazilian culture brought happiness and began to attract the attention of the press, gaining public contact. As a result, this culture found its niche in Brazil's white African areas, as well as in areas populated by white non-Africans, who now continued to be top dog.

The rich attended the biggest, and oldest, *Casas de Santo* in Bahia, to study Candomblé and Umbanda, whilst the poor would go to polar opposite institutions.

In the big, *Casas de Santo*, the poor had space to help develop the *axé*, force. They left photographs in the photo-album and made interviews available to anthropologists and artists, the rich and famous. The number of books devoted to the field grew in universities and in bookshops. Those who were able to understand the book openly believed that they knew enough about, and were capable of teaching about, energy and the Orishas.

The fact is that, for those poor people who do not know

about the African culture and religion, Umbanda remained.

In African religion, the Orishas are mother energies that flow through nature. The oceans, the rivers, the earth, fire and clouds are all living entities that, once aligned with human instinct, help man connect with all that is divine.

This connection is a secret art, much the same as other alchemic sciences. African alchemic science is similar to Asclepius', Theophrastus' and Empedocles' studies, in Greece. It is equally similar to Paracelsus', Rudolph Steiner's and Hahnemann's studies in Europe. This secret African art has a beautiful, and spontaneous, ritual which bears resemblance to Dionysian dances. However, this art forms part of an intrinsic secret that relates to any and all art, culture or science that aims to preserve itself against consumerist and superficial manipulation, for they are blemishes that stain the real beauty that can be found in the books and papers that are believed, by intellectuals, to tell nothing but the truth.

In Umbanda, San Antonio is either Ogum or Oxossi, depending on the State where he is being discussed. Iansa is Saint Barbara. In Umbanda, the Orishas may be consulted. They communicate with humans, which is something that is different to the Candomblé. What's more, it is completely different to the science that Mel learnt from Mãe Helena and from Pai Damásio.

Mel frightened herself when she entered Maria's Umbanda Centre. Plastic skeletons, raw meat and bottles of sugar cane brandy... Everything was very dirty. There were black and red capes and odalisque clothes...

"Maria, what is all this?"

"We have to make it look impressive, don't we?! If we don't, then the money doesn't come in. People want to be frightened; they need panic and fear. If you can give that to them, they will pay anything you want and who are they to bargain?"

"You're right about that."

Mel quickly assessed her options:

*Option 1:*

Move back in with Bida.
Pros: contact with the Partisan struggle; freedom of religious

choice.

Cons: Bida's changed. He currently lives with left-wing radicals and Mel had no desire to associate herself with them.

*Option 2:*

Return to Bahia.

Pros: Mel searched long and hard for a plus point but found none.

Cons: fights with her father, repression of thought; something that would prevent Mel from living. The freedom to think was part of her very being, as was the freedom to express and carry out those same thoughts.

*Option 3:*

Live in Maria's Umbanda Centre.

Cons: live with skeletons, black capes and a large number of spirits that haven't accepted death and who cling to this world (spirits who acted out the most heinous of human behaviours) who would often hurt Mel.

Pros: to be able to stop looking for somewhere to live, to get out of the cold, in the expensive State of São Paulo.

"Here you only need to work to be able to afford food. Talking of which; the money you earn from doing market research, does it pay you enough to feed yourself?"

Mel looked at Maria and thought: "I wonder what she calls 'feeding yourself?"

When she lived with her family in Bahia, Mel's knowledge of food extended to meat, fish, chicken, seafood, vegetables, lentils, milk, bread and cheese, etc.

Whilst she was living in the street as a trucker, Mel learnt to cook *"arroz oleo de freio"*, a rice dish commonly made by truckers where the rice is stuffed with cheese. The sounds made as the cheese melted and blistered in the hot pan resembled the noises made by the truck when she was still on the road, just obviously on a smaller scale. This was *arroz oleo de freio*.

Mel, when she was still in her Macarrão phase, learnt how to cook other dishes also, each one with the same skill and finesse.

After she had gone to live with Bida, Mel learnt to eat green banana soup, as well as how not to eat; to suppress the feeling of being hungry; the pangs that come from having an empty stomach and the inability to think when the body becomes weak because of the lack of protein.

"I make money, yes, Maria and the earnings are sufficient to be able to feed myself, whether it be with food in the times of plenty, or the spirit when times are hard."

"You talk oddly, child."

"I know, Maria. People have always said this."

"So? Will you stay or won't you?"

Mel stayed and made a conscious effort to thank God for watching over her. That said, she would prefer to live in a house with a mother and father who understood and could help her discover her *raison d'être*, her purpose in the world. Mel wanted gardens in which to grow flowers and learn how to 'grow' thorny plants, like the rose, to safeguard herself throughout life. Many people believe they know the pain of being pricked by roses, just because they grow roses in their gardens. Mel had already read about this. She would have loved to have learned more like this: coming to grips with, and learning about, life including its pains, dangers, loves, joys and secrets, all whilst just sitting there in the garden, reading books written by famous authors. Mel wanted all of this. Wasn't this the way, after all, that her friends learnt? It seemed enough to just read a book and there you'd have it!

Mel envied the round glasses fashioned by the pacifist intellectuals: "Imagine peace. Imagine a nation without religion, without borders, without flags. Imagine light fading and entering our bodies. Imagine being in a dark place. Imagine untying your tie. Imagine being on the other side, where the grass is greener."

Everything Mel had learnt was sound, in black and white, in pain and love, light and shadow. It was all real, all true.

"I'm going to stay here, Maria."

Mel left in the early hours. She needed to be at either the *Avenida Paulista* or *Faria Lima* at 8am, to be able to collect the questionnaires she needed to conduct the market research. She caught the train at 6am and alighted at the *Estação da luz*. From there, she caught the bus.

By doing this work in São Paulo, Mel learnt the temperament of the *Paulistanos:*

"I don't have time to answer your questions. I'm in a rush; now's not a good time!"

"Excuse me madam. I just have a few questions about margarine that I'd like to ask you, if you have time, with the aim of making the manufacturer listen more to your needs." explained Mel, in an attempt to finish the questionnaires with factual information that she could submit to her bosses. Mel insisted on finishing all her questionnaires, so that she could pay her way in Maria's Umbanda Centre.

Mel understood that she was more than just one person at the same time, as she took on two personalities simultaneously: Mel, a competent worker employed by a company and Mel, a needy and deprived adolescent who was battling, working herself into the ground to prevent herself from becoming a 'pariah'.

Mel arrived home. Home? She arrived at Maria's Umbanda Centre sometime between half-past midnight and one in the morning, and went straight up to bed. Bed?

*"Oi girl, do you live here too? Do me a favour and open that bottle of rum, I'm parched!"*

"You're not a real person; why do you want to drink rum?"

*"I have to have a drink; my mouth is like a desert!"*

"No, I'm not going to open the bottle for you. You don't belong to the material world anymore."

*"Fine, then you'll have to drink it for me, or has Maria still not shown you how to do this?"*

"I don't know anything about Maria's work. Let me sleep; I need to get up early in the morning."

*"Everyone who is here with me knows that you can see, here and feel our presence."*

Mel needed to break off from these spirit entities, who were completely unhinged, so that she could get some rest.

One day...

"Maria, do you see, and hear, these spirits that you respect so much?"

"I don't see anything. But when they appear, I am taken completely by their consciousness."

"Maria, I'm a medium with knowledge of Afro-Brazilian religion and, where I come from, we work in a very different way to you."

"Really? I have been to Salvador. It was very difficult to get an interview or appointment with the head priests and priestesses, Babalorixas and Ialorixas, there. I know that the spirits that take me over attract clients and I don't go hungry. On the contrary, I actually make a good living."

Mel accompanied Maria to work every Saturday from that point on. She ceased working with the questionnaires on these days, given that all she would hear from potential candidates was:

"I'm going to the cinema; now's not a good time."

"I'm on my way into town; another time."

This time, Mel watched as Maria manifested the spirits that helped clients:

"You're Glicério. Your boss is called Ricardo, correct?"

"Yes, yes he is." replied the tanned man, innocence radiating out of every pore of his body.

"Oh, my child. This Ricardo, your boss, has sent a 'macumba', a curse of sorts, to kill you. The 'macumba' must be undone!"

The spirit smoked a cigar, which poked out the side of its mouth, with smoke dancing on its tongue, pirouetting, before continuing to terrify the client before him:

"This 'macumba' must be stopped, otherwise you'll die! You're going to die, you're going to die, you're going to die! I am 'Sete Facadas', your friend and guardian. For 700 in notes, I'll undo the 'macumba'."

With these episodes, Mel learnt what tragicomic meant. It was a phrase she first came across when reading a journal, where a film critic said:

"It's a tragic comedy and makes use of black humour."

People go to the cinema and, it's by doing this, that they learn what a tragicomic episode is.

For Mel, it was different. She learnt what tragicomic was by living with Maria and her 'helping spirits', in a Casa de Umbanda in Poá, on the outskirts of São Paulo.

The following Saturday, there was another tragicomic episode that came about from an incident involving corruption. This time, the spirits were intentionally deceptive and shamelessly abused the faith put in them by the public:

"You are Ricardo. I can see an employee of yours, Glicério, plotting against you. He wants your job. Oh, my child, he wants you dead and has been driven mad by his own ambition."

Mel sat there, more afraid than all the rest combined! From being a seer, Mel knew what was happening and could see 'Sete Facadas' take over Maria da Luz's body and mind.

"What do I do?!?... Should I report the charlatan to the authorities?" thought the activist, and politically correct, Mel.

"This woman needs to make a living." thought another side of Mel, who knew all too well how difficult and arduous it was to earn a crust.

During the conflict, the side to Mel that stands by the truth emerged victorious.

The following Saturday:

"Mr Glicério, I need to talk to you. My name is Mel. Do you have a boss called Ricardo? You don't need to reply; it was rhetorical. I know you do. He was here last week. If I'm honest, you came one Saturday and he came the other. You've been turned into enemies by a spirit that calls itself 'Sete Facadas'. Of the two of you, you and Ricardo that is, I preferred talking to you."

Mel said everything she was able to, as well as those things she struggled to say. Mr Glicério just stood in silence, looking at his wife.

The conversation was over quickly. Maria wasn't going to be long before getting in… and, true to form, she wasn't.

"Get the hell out of my house; get out! I warned you not to meddle in my business. You have five minutes to get the hell out of my Centre!" she shrieked, storming off.

"*Go with Mr Glicério.*" Mel's spirit friend instructed, surprising her with the advice.

The scene I recall from when Mel was leaving Maria's Centre

was rather sad yet, at the same time, hopeful. Every 200 metres or so, Mr Glicério and his wife, Nilza, would look back and see Mel there with her rucksacks. The couple stopped at a snack bar. Mel watched them from the other side of the road.

"Come here. Come sit with us."

Four soft drinks and several cakes later, Mel had managed to recount her entire story, right back from when she left Bahia and her parents, onwards to the couple. She told them about her time with Bida and her brief stay at Maria's Centre. Mr Glicério was also from the Sertão in Bahia.

I wonder if it's possible for someone to learn about a *Sertanejo*'s life, just from reading books? No, I don't think it is. At best, the reader will just have a vague idea; at worst, they will just assume that everything about the place is fiction. I don't believe that it is possible for someone to learn all there is about theory, without getting stuck into the practical side also. Books inspire us; they open doors for our imagination and creativity. For this reason, I'm not going to write about life back in Brazil's Sertão.

The fact is that Mr Glicério listened in silence to the story that Mel was telling him. He knew it was the truth. He understood the brutality that comes from a lack of understanding.

"I'm shocked. I allowed Maria to deceive me. Ricardo and I are to blame. If we had only talked about our differences, none of this would have happened. Do you have anywhere to go?"

"Oh yes, I just don't know where it is yet." responded an ever hopeful Mel.

Mr Glicério and Nilza exchanged a look briefly, before he spoke:

"Let's head home. Do you know how to cook, Mel? I bet it's been what seems like a lifetime since you last ate *feijão da Bahia*? We'll think about the rest later."

Nilza was a *Paulista* but, in reality, seemed closer to a *Baiana*, more so than any other *Paulista* Mel had ever met. A characteristic of the people from Bahia is that they attempt to resolve problems with a light-heartedness and parties.

The three of them walked together, completely content. Anyone seeing them would, without doubt, have taken them to be a family. Mr Glicério and Nilza did everything in their power to help Mel. It had been more than a year since Mel had lived in a harmonious and happy home, where there was a mother and father, love and protection.

Their home was simplistic with two rooms, a small living room and a bathroom. They had two young children, Rosângela and Ronaldo. Glicério's parents lived in an annexe.

Mel lived there for about a year. She became a jack-of-all-trades; she worked as a cleaner, a fruit seller, a shoeshine, a coffee seller, etc.

She tried to work in a factory, but it didn't work out. Mel was still a revolutionary for the working class cause. She was almost happy. She didn't talk about her family any more, nor about the past. 'Never look back'. It was a cliché used by many of the left-wing, pseudo-revolutionary Brazilian singers she listened to.

If ever someone did ask her about the past, she simply ended the conversation before it had even begun:

"How much of a past can a 17 year old have?" was her favourite response.

Her spirit friends taught her to make certain teas, baths and to carry out certain therapeutic practices that helped to improve Mr Glicério's health. He was already on the mend, given that his illness hadn't come about as a result of sorcery, *ebos* and black magic.

Did I say therapeutic practices?... Yes, yes I did! Mel had no idea that her new knowledge was the start of a type of therapy that she was going to use, as Halu Gamashi, to help patients and other therapists who were interested in a 'light' and functional medicine.

Mel practiced her 'science' freely, fluidly. It was good for Mr. Guilinho: Mr. Glicério's nickname. When he was healed, other people in need of healing came from all around *São Paulo*. So what did Mel do? She helped them, with no assistance from traditional medicine.

"Everything I know about this, I learnt from the spirits. I see the dead as though they were still among the living."

"Are they good spirits?" the people would ask Mel.

"Are they like the spirits that Maria da Luz uses? Are they the same spirits?"

"No, no they aren't. They are different. They don't try to deceive, nor do they discriminate. They teach me how to cure the sick." Mel replied. She was still so young, not even 17 at this point, and didn't have the faintest idea of what other people called 'good':

"The good I pass on through my knowledge…" repeated one of Mel's teachers, who used to make a habit of looking at the breasts of the girls in the school.

"My thinking is completely lucid!" Mel's father used to prattle on.

"The light from my spirit contacts will help you…" were the words that were written on Maria's business cards.

Even today, neither Mel nor Halu Gamashi understand what other people consider to be good and light.

Mel never made business cards, nor did she ever open up a Centre for people to go to. She could hardly close the door to the small room she lived out of when some poor, destitute soul came knocking, asking for her help:

"It's like this Ms Zefa. I know what I do because of the spirits. I'm going to help you, but that doesn't mean that you should stop going to see your doctor."

"What doctor, child? I don't have a GP, nor do I have any health service documentation. Will you help me? I need the help. I asked God for guidance and he led me to you."

In a way, Ms Zefa reminded me of Mãe Helena. She was humble and had a knowledge of how to understand complex topics.

Nowadays, when the then Mel, now Halu Gamashi, is questioned about her knowledge, she responds by writing books, giving lectures and offering courses. She aims to find and prove her knowledge to the public, who need to understand that there is 'light' and science behind what she says.

But even now, Halu Gamashi knows that the explanation that Ms Zefa gave was the most correct and eloquent: "I need the help. I asked God to guide me and he led me to you."

Halu Gamashi believes that the explanation given by Ms Zefa is the most correct for any type of healer, whether traditional or alternative.

Mel continued to help her 'patients':

"No, Guilherme. I still don't charge for my services. I'm still learning."

"Well then; it's a gift. Surely you can accept that?"

"It's a gift in exchange for the service that I'm providing?"

"Exactly!"

"I'm afraid not, then. You'd still be paying me for the service."

Mel lived on the small services she provided, like cleaning, selling fruit and coffee, etc. Where she didn't have the means to be able to attend formal institutions, she studied in unofficial schools, where the teachers were not legally teachers in the eyes of the law, and where she was able to debate with others like herself; people who weren't counted in IBGE statistics.

"Do you think they are going to come, Glicério? Do you think they will come to speak to us?"

It was that time again to fill in the census. Mel knew well what people meant when they talked about the census. She had learnt about it by watching TV at Glicério's house. As she knew that not everyone was fortunate enough to have a TV, Mel took it upon herself to spread the word. After work, a euphoric Mel set out, encouraged by the report she had heard in the break between news bulletins.

"Ms Marinalva, come here please… a very important person will come to your house. He's a census officer."

"Is that really what he is called? How odd!"

"A census officer is the title given to the person who has to come round and count how many people are in each of the houses in Brazil. The census is done to help improve people's lives, Ms Marinalva. It helps poor people, like us, the most. Because of this, it is important that you let these people, these census officers, into your home. They will ask you questions. If you don't understand the question, ask them to explain themselves another way. You mustn't give them wrong information, otherwise it complicates things."

Mel spread this message to all those who either completely, or partially, didn't understand what they had heard, as well as to those who were worried.

"Glicério, they need to understand more about the census. On the TV they said that they want to know how many people there are in Brazil. Then, based on what they find out, they are going to build more hospitals and schools, etc."

"Mel, can you help me with your 'techniques'? My back is hurting and my hand has started to tingle again."

"Sir, you've spent so long not letting me help you. I told you there was still work to do."

"I said not to help me because I didn't want to put you out. Don't expect much from this census."

But Mel waited for them. She set up camp in the nearby streets, waiting for census officers to come… but they never did.

"And now, Glicério, how are they going to know that there are so many destitute people here in *Ferraz de Vasconcelos*?"

"By looking at statistics. They'll know. The moment that the poor and destitute disappear, so does their good life." responded a man from the Sertão.

This is how Mel lived this part of her life. From here on in, she lived to learn and studied through her seeing abilities.

"I see and hear the spirits of those who have passed as if they were still among the living." This explained everything for Mel. It made everything crystal clear and lucid.

# Mercinha

The day had arrived for Mel to return home, to her family. At this time in her life, she still hadn't learnt about the 'margins of time' and how these are ruled by our feelings of nostalgia.

The idea to return came to Mel in a dream. She dreamt about her Grandmother, Dulce, bidding her farewell. She woke up in tears, feeling home-sick and missing her brothers, her mother, even her father. She told Nilza about the dream and took counsel from her about how best to move forward:

"Call them, Mel. Look for your family. You're suffering from destitution here with us and they seem to be doing ok. You left home, you lived away. Go back; it'll be different this time."

Mel returned. She started her journey home by phoning her family. She said her goodbyes and left. A few tears were shed, but the thought of seeing her family brought her a happiness that choked back the tears and the memories.

When she arrived home, there were tears, celebrations and hugs. Even her father hugged her. Even he celebrated her return. Mel lived her fifteen minutes of fame, but this ended as it had come. It ended the next day:

"You are a wretch! You have tarnished the good name of this family. Do you have any idea how many stories we had to make up to explain your disappearance? Yesterday, after the party, I stopped to think and it dawned on me that you didn't deserve the celebration. We only celebrated because of your mother and brothers. I'm gonna knock you into next week, you God-damn, miserable wretch!"

This is how Mel died…but what name was she going to go by now?

"Open the door, Mercinha! Your father really has gone mad. He's lost it. It's me, your auntie. I wasn't able to make it to the party yesterday."

This is how Mercinha was born; in the rain, beaten black and blue, broken as much on the inside as the out. She walked out the bathroom, grabbed her rucksack and fled again.

She thought about running back to São Paulo, to *Ferraz*, but decided against it. She felt drained, exhausted. It was only 24 hours since she had left there.

She decided to stay. She tracked down a friend from days gone by, moved in with her and started work in an insurance company. Turunga had grown up and become Mercinha.

They say a picture is worth a thousand words. Mercinha was the living embodiment of these words. She was the polar opposite to Mel. The rebellious side had grown. She asked the spirits, her teachers, to keep their distance:

"Leave! Go away! I've had enough! Leave me in peace! I don't want this anymore!"

Mercinha needed to blame someone for her poor family relations. She needed to blame someone for the difficulties encountered throughout her life for being 'different'. But it was more than this. Mercinha needed to curse, offend, pummel and get back at life… she needed to rip the violent scars from her body, fighting fire with fire and the only way to do this was to use the language of violence.

Mercinha needed to be violent. She allowed the meeker side of herself to surface. Whether consciously, or subconsciously, Mercinha knew that, if she gave as many scars as she had to those who had scarred her, she would be marooned in her intention. Yes, she would hurt them, but she would come out more isolated and even more scarred. Whether consciously, or subconsciously, she allowed the meeker sides of herself to surface, safe in the knowledge that they themselves would not resort to fighting fire with fire, using the language of violence.

She let her hair grow and changed the way in which she

dressed. She went into a little thrift shop and bought a black leather jacket and trousers, and orange leather boots. She lived in these clothes and only changed them when they were beyond dirty. When they did reach this state, Mercinha would swap them for another pair of well-worn jeans and denim jacket, purchased in the same little thrift shop.

Mercinha worked by selling motor and life insurance. Ironically, an insecure Mercinha was assuring her clients of the importance of having insurance. One of her favourite phrases was: "Whoever said that life was fair?" Having insurance can guarantee peace of mind for when life's troubles come knocking at our door and you have nowhere else to turn.

Mercinha also sold trust funds for vehicles, televisions and microwaves. "Whoever said that life was fair?" Purchasing these licences was the only way that the poor, and destitute, could have one of the comforts that the rich took for granted.

"Get a group of twenty to forty poor, and destitute, people together. Each one of them joins the association with a small amount of money and there come the funds for the trust. By joining these associations, the poor are able to win money and so able to have the same kinds of things rich people have. In the end, everyone walks away with their profit; the only difference between them is when."

She continued:

"This is the only way the poor can be lucky. Do you want to miss this chance?"

Mercinha sold trust funds to supplement her income. Given how hard times were, she also sold costume jewellery, voucher booklets and scratch cards and also filters for sparkling water.

Back around this time, Mercinha had the nickname 'Mary Help'. One of her brothers only ever called her this, as every time someone saw her she would try and sell them something that she thought may help them in one way or another.

"Here comes Mary Help! Run guys! If you don't, she'll sell you something."

"Guys, have you heard of the "Igloo"? It's a hotel chain for the poor. They say you can find them across Brazil. I have some details here to show you. They are little houses that look like simple little Eskimo igloos. It's a set up to trick the poor. I don't know if it's legal, but it's a nice idea for the poor to be able to travel and pay reduced prices. I'd have thought that they'd be crappy… but it's a way to travel!"

Mel sold so many shares for this particular product.

"I am 18 years old. I've already lived a damn sight more than many people in their 60's. I've already seen a lot in my life. I'm no longer under any illusion. Why should I cry? If you cry, the pain you feel comes face to face with a beast that you won't be able to shake. If you resist the urge, and hold back the tears, the pain fades and goes, searching for another beast to cling to."

Mercinha was like this. On the one hand, an antithesis of Turunga. On the other, on a deeper level, she was the same girl that had once been upset at her balloons flying away. Turunga didn't cry. Her uncle had told her that this could happen if she didn't tie her balloons to something weighty. As Turunga didn't want to tie her balloons up, she had to grieve their loss as they flew away. She didn't cry as she didn't want to give her uncle the satisfaction of knowing he had upset her, as he laughed about her loss as he stood before her.

Mercinha had other balloons, but they were the same nonetheless. They flew away, they didn't stay. Friends came and went, as is normal in life. They went to university, to weddings, to dress fittings…

Mercinha discovered poverty and destitution were rife in the outskirts of Salvador and other neighbouring cities. She sold trust funds and costume jewellery. Two days were never the same. She didn't want to stay put, set up roots. She was afraid of enjoying herself, of falling in love and being dependent. Every day she was in a new place with new, and different, friends and temporary friendships. There were parties, so many parties. When she serenaded people, she discovered that she had a reasonable voice, found by some to be pleasing and by others to be annoying. She became a night owl and started singing in small bars:

"Will this be enough for me to make rent? I do what I enjoy and still manage to make some money."

Mercinha had 'lovers'. Do you know what they are? Friends whose paths crossed Mercinha's, who came into her life and who lived intimately, and profoundly, in her experiences, her comedy and her gift. These friendships were filled with such deep, and intense, emotions that anyone looking from the outside in would often mistake the friendship for more. This coexistence with these friends was intense, profound and short-lived:

"Mercinha, I need to return to reality."

"Go on mate; it's your turn."

"Come with me; come and live in my house. I'll ask my father to see if he can give you a permanent job."

Part of Mercinha wanted to go, but a larger part didn't... it wouldn't allow her to. There were new friends, new adventures, journeys, opportunities to learn, sunsets, paths to follow.

As much as Mercinha didn't want to, she couldn't bring herself to turn people in need away. She hadn't forgotten what she had learnt as Mel. She made use of the 'techniques' she had picked up. She taught how to make the teas and the baths. She didn't want to, yet she helped people. In this irony, Mercinha discovered a way of helping people without subjugating herself completely:

"You know what? I know a lot about a lot of things, some of which are not widely known. I used to work for other people, but I'm not going to talk much about this. I don't want to. What I really want is to forget this part of me. Don't ask me anything else about it because I'm not going to answer. I'll find a way to rid you of this sickness. If you want to try..."

"If you tell me more about it, it might be something I could try..."

"Never mind. Forget it."

"Erm... sorry; I understand you don't want to talk about it. So, even though you're a little out there, I consider you to be a trustworthy person."

"A little out there?"

"You know... part hippie, part politician, part prophet and a friend."

This summed Mercinha up. She was made up of different parts, pieces, leftovers that just wouldn't go away. A whole body will perform; for example, a serious face combined with a suit and tie or tux. She had a serious face. She spoke with a serious edge to her voice, in a tone that made people understand she knew what she was talking about. She talked using slang and idioms, dressed in leather and wearing sandals that stunk, bought at the Mercado Modelo, a huge and intensely popular market in Salvador.

One day, someone said to her:

"You're so different behind closed doors."

"To the world, physically, you look bloody mad: nuts, hippie, insane. On the inside, however, you're wise, intelligent and true. You've heard the story: *The Prince and the Pauper*, right? It's a film that shows two people who are very similar physically, yet who have completely opposite backgrounds."

Mercinha loved intelligent chat and would go to bars where poetry was recited, and music sung, in search of it. The absence of fame was suffocated by raw talent, untainted voices and poems by singers in the bohemian night. Such was the more secretive, underground, life on the streets of Salvador.

"Drunks, druggies, pederasts and whores. She prefers to live with these people. She doesn't know what it is to live with a family." said her father contemptuously in an attempt to justify Mercinha's absences at the table to the rest of the guests as well as, at the same time, explaining Mercinha's presence in the life that she chose.

However, the poetry and the songs of the bars drowned out Mercinha's pains. She discovered that sharing the pain refined the ego.

None of Mercinha's friends felt uncomfortable by the fact that she was different:

"Oi, Mercinha, who are you talking to?"

"Hun, can't you see who I'm talking to?"

"No, there is no-one sat at the table with you."

"Yes there is. You just can't see them! Now that you've made comment, I know that I am talking to a spirit."

"Aren't you afraid?"

"Of what? The spirit's telling me stories. The spirits that dwell in bars need the energy from the alcohol and the smoke. From this, they are able to satisfy the density and the unbalance in their ethereal bodies. They are consciousnesses that are dependent on the density of the world. Who knows, one day might we not be like them?"

"Even knowing this, you're here in the bar?!?"

"I come here because I depend on hearing poetry and feeling accepted. Cigars and beer are part of the atmosphere, it would be foolish to think otherwise and useless to fight for them not to be consumed here. When I get home, I take a herbal bath, to cleanse, just as I have been taught."

"So, teach us some of these things you know!"

Mercinha taught them. The next time they met:

"Christ, sweetie! It was worth it! I think I've actually started to drink less. It's a good thing that you're here. Who else would come here to clean up a little of the crap?"

No-one called her mad. There was no discrimination among the rebels. None whatsoever. The rebels only discriminated between stuck up daddies' little girls and posh, "I'm so much better than you" lads and their traditional, formal way of fitting into society, which the rebels could not abide to be associated with.

Time went by. One day, Mercinha woke up and remembered Mr Humberto, the man who had helped her twice and who had introduced her to Mãe Helena and Pai Damásio.

"I need to find him; it's time."

She was certain of it. It was the silent drive that Turunga, and Mel, had both felt, that now stirred within Mercinha.

She knew how to contact Mr Humberto, despite not knowing his telephone number. She knew roughly what his address was. He lived in Acupe de Brotas, one of the districts in Salvador.

"Which was his street? I know, I'll just follow my gut. I'll go where my instinct leads me."

"Mr Humberto, do you remember me?"

"Come in, my child. I always knew that I would see you again. Your mother once came to me and said that you had run away from home. Come in, come in. Sit down and have some water."

Tears welled in Mercinha's eyes, before trickling down her cheeks. She sat on the sofa and broke down completely. She purged herself of her childhood pains through her tears. She poured her heart out to Mr Humberto, who just sat there listening patiently to her.

In that moment, Mercinha discovered that, as much as she had tried to distance herself from the pain, the pain had never truly left her. She was surprised at how much she cried. Mr Humberto, however, wasn't. As Mercinha started to compose herself, Mr Humberto said:

"I knew, I knew. Bessem is the energy in nature that wisdom is made of. In this world, in order to become wise, one must first walk a long road many times. Bessem is the energy from nature that strengthens our souls so that we are able to complete our tasks. How old are you now?"

"Coming up to 19."

"On the subject of coming and going; today marks the start of a new chapter in your life. Will you continue to heed my counsel?"

Of course she would. Mercinha knew that she was there to listen to how to proceed on this new journey. She was happy. Unlike Mel; Mercinha died happy.

The day the incarnation of Mercinha died was the day on which she felt happiest. It took place when, six months after this visit, she was finally accepted as a charge, a student named Iaô, in the house of Nidê. Nidê was another keeper of the energies of nature. He belonged to the same group, and the same way of thinking, as Mãe Helena and Pai Damásio. Mercinha died happy, after a short life spanning less than a year. So what name would she go by now?

"Iaô, are you giving it zeds? Did you get me the water from the fountain I asked you for?"

Mercinha was born in the shower. Iaô was born in the Oxum fountain on Nidê's estate. Iaô is the title given to someone who is a new recruit into the Afro-Brazilian sect.

"I know that you started to refine your energies and were initiated when you were 12. I was told, in great detail, about you by Helena. At the age of 14, you spent a mandatory year with Damásio. You learnt a great deal from them, but you still have no idea how much you have left, and how much you need, to learn."

Nidê put up such a fight not to take on Mercinha. The reason for his reluctance was only to come to light years later.

Mercinha had set out immediately, from Mr Damásio's home, to find Nidê.

"Go, my child. I'll call Nidê. He's not someone who can be called flexible, by any stretch of the imagination. He's completely the opposite, in fact. He's reserved because he knows the sacred power contained within his knowledge and practices. We live in hard times. Every day, metaphysical and extrasensory studies are made more superficial. They are made into entertainment programmes on the television and are used as a tourist attraction for outsiders. Nidê is against all of this. For this reason, he is one of those people who believes in the fundamentals of an idea but who doesn't agree with the way in which the idea, in this case of traditional Candomblé, is carried out and implemented. Don't forget, he is the best-suited person to take care of you."

Safe in this knowledge, Mercinha set out to find him. He lived in an estate somewhere between Itapuã and São Cristóvão.

"Please, may I speak to Mr Nidê?"

Mercinha arrived at the estate, walked through the gate and found Mr Nidê. He was short, though would have been considered of average height in *Bahia*, where men aren't particularly tall in comparison to the Paulistas that Mel had met.

Nidê was like this: about 5 ft 2 inches tall, deep blue eyes and white hair, although you could see that he had been blonde when he was younger.

Mercinha hadn't met many keepers of the Orishas, but those that she either knew in person, or through the media, were ethnic in origin.

"Who's looking for him?"

"I'm the girl that Mr Humberto spoke to you about."

"Come back on Saturday."

"On Saturday?!? Today is Thursday…"

"Are you deaf? Come back on Saturday."

Speechless, Mercinha left. She thought about going back and looking for Mr Humberto. She thought about giving up, but decided against it on both counts. Instead, she returned to the estate on Saturday:

"Pai Nidê. I'm the girl that was here on Thursday…"

He interrupted:

"Come back on Tuesday."

So she did. On Tuesday when she returned, he said:

"Come back on Thursday."

Come back on Tuesday; come back on Thursday; come back on Saturday... this continued for six months, with the same promise of teaching a few days later being given each time.

But for the fact she had that voice inside her telling her to not give up, Mercinha would have stopped trying. For six months, Mercinha was unable to get more than five words out herself before Nidê would cut across her and give her the three words, as always.

Six months later, on a Saturday, Mercinha was invited out with a friend:

"Mercinha, do you want to come with me to the Island? Monday is a bank holiday. We will have plenty of time to enjoy the beach ."

"Jonga, if I could I would but today is Saturday. I need to go to Pai Nidê's estate."

"You're still going to see that old man? Can't you see that the man doesn't want to help you? Face it, Mercinha, give up... otherwise you'll have to make your own way to São Cristóvão, and it's a distance. Nidê is a waste of time! You know he's not going to see you."

"He's going to need to be the one to tell me this. That's the only way that I'm going to give up. If he doesn't, then I'll continue to do what he says. You have a car. We'll go there quickly. If he tells me to come back next week, on Tuesday, then we'll go to the island."

The island Mercinha and Jonga were wanting to go to was the Island of Itaparica, where Cacha Pregos beach is. This beach is of great importance for Turunga, Mel, Mercinha, Iaô and Halu Gamashi.

# Iaô

This chapter was written in Cacha Pregos, on 14<sup>th</sup> January 2004, at 6:08pm, Bahia time. In other Brazilian states, it would have been 7:08pm, because of the time difference; another tool used by the Government to save energy.

I look towards the ocean, which now shimmers silver with the light reflected from the ashy sky and clouds. A good friend of mine listens to me and writes down my memories in a notebook, there to be kept for all time. I would never suggest using a computer. He knows that I don't like them. On the neighbouring veranda, I can hear the voices of some life-long friends and companions, who have stood by me throughout my fight and by whom I have stood when they, in turn, have had their hard times.

Other friends are also here. We are all together, taking a trip down memory lane, revisiting hard times that, I thank God, the Orishas and my spirit friends, are far behind me now. I'll call everyone later. And one of my friends will read over what has been written.

There are still some people who are yet to arrive. I look out for them in the beautiful Cacha Pregos, the idyllic beach on which Mercinha and Jonga longed to spend a final week. I don't remember now which holiday it was in Bahia; there are, after all, so many… Bahia!

\* \* \*

"It's not going to take long, is it, Mercinha?"

"No, hun. The man won't let me get more than a few words out. I'll listen to the three words he has to say to me, then will come back and find you here and we'll go to the island."

Jonga stopped the car three hundred metres or so distance from the gate.

"Pai Nidê, it's me again."

"Yesterday we had a party. Go to the kitchen and bring out desserts and refreshments for the people who are waiting to be served."

"Mr Nidê, you're talking to me?" Mercinha asked, surprised.

"Is there someone else here with us?"

"Mr Nidê, let me get this straight. You're sending me to the kitchen to bring out, and serve, desserts and refreshments?"

"That's correct."

"Where is your kitchen?"

"Oh Lord, that's what I was forgetting! Does your house have a kitchen?"

"Erm… yes…"

"What is the kitchen like in your house?"

"Well, it has a fridge, an oven…"

"Mine has these things too."

"And cups and plates; where are they?"

"In the bathroom, in the toilet. Do you not keep them there then?!?"

Baffled. Mercinha felt completely baffled as she went in search of the desserts. She had completely forgotten about Jonga and the island. One hour later, tired of waiting for her, Jonga came onto the estate. Once inside, he found Nidê, who politely welcomed him inside. Mercinha found out about this meeting a week later, when she met up with Jonga again.

"Mercinha, you're mad! You said that the old man was hostile and anti-social. He wasn't; he was really nice. He invited me in, gave me a beer and made small talk with me whilst you were inside the house."

Mercinha was completely confused by what she heard.

"You met Pai Nidê?"

"Did he not tell you? What do you talk about?"

Mercinha told Jonga about the cake, the desserts and the refreshments and talked him through it all, step by step.

"After I served desserts and refreshments, Pai Nidê called me over to talk to him. He said: 'Child, you have a lot of work ahead of you. You have passed the first test. You are determined. I'm yet to see, however, if your determination will be sufficient for you to be able to learn what you need to learn, to get through what you need to get through.'"

"Could you tell me a bit more about this?"

"Everything in time. For now, you're not going to say anything; rather you're going to listen to my requirements. You will listen to what I have to say and then go away and think about what I have said. If you accept what I say, stick some money in your rucksack and come back on Tuesday."

"I left the estate, Jonga, but I couldn't find you … I caught a bus and went home to auntie. I grabbed some money and went back on Tuesday. I only left yesterday, Friday, in the evening. During that whole time, Pai Nidê never said anything to me about you two having met. I was inside, having a bath in herbs. I assumed you had given up waiting and headed over to the island."

"Mercinha, are you sure you want to get involved with these people? These people are weird, full of secrets and deal with the occult."

This didn't deter Mercinha. The following Tuesday, she continued with her treatment in Pai Nidê's house.

Mercinha started to take more baths and cleansings using different herbs and, in them, made increasing use of vegetables and lentils. All this Afro-Brazilian scientific alchemy caused her to have a radiant glow. Mercinha learnt other chants, to invoke the spirits. She learnt to devote her body, and soul, to the energies in nature. She underwent sacred rituals. She slept on a mat on the floor, amongst the rest of the furnishings. She opened the *Igba*, she gave *Dubali* in the *Peji*, and learnt to beat *Paó*.

"*Orroboboia*, Bessem! *Orroboboia!*" Greetings to the Bessem Orisha.

Mercinha gave continuity to her initiation. As I already said,

Mercinha died happy. She died happy at the end of her mad, lunatic, hippie life and was reborn in the sacred hand of Pai Nidê, on the mat: Iaô de Bessem.

"Iaô, have you washed Yemanjá's room yet? What about tidying Ogum's room? And the Xango's okra, have you made the *amalá*? Are Ibeji's pots washed? The ones that are used for the Orisha rituals? Iaô, have you prayed? Go and pray, child. Pray for strength and enlightenment."

Iaô was born happy. She was happy all of the time. She found a new sense of being accepted. Her energies were balanced and harmonious. She lost the desire to drink beer and cut down the number of cigars she smoked.

"Pai Nidê, is drinking and smoking wrong?"

"Yes, they're bad for your health."

"So aren't you going to tell me to stop drinking and smoking?"

"I will but, in my own way. I'll keep looking after your energies and make sure that your natural energy flow is kept balanced and pure. From there, this compulsion to drink and smoke will pass. That doesn't mean that you're going to stop; that will be down to you. Instead, the reasons compelling you to smoke and drink will be eliminated."

He continued to explain:

"It's common for people with your sensitivity to need to build up energy and to look for false stability. It's like being clean in a filthy house. You make yourself dirty so that you are like the house. Becoming dirty, in my example, is the compulsion that you're trying to rid yourself of."

"Pai Nidê, I've only been drunk once," Iaô explained, so that he didn't have the wrong idea about her.

"Stop justifying yourself. I'm not accusing you of anything. The life that you brought with you from when you were growing up with your father has made you now defend yourself constantly. Time will bring maturity and it will free you from your need to do this. Now that we have mentioned your father; how is he?"

"I don't know, Pai Nidê. Ever since I decided to come to your house, our relationship has become almost non-existent. I grew tired of his mockery. I couldn't stand listening to him call the Orishas for livestock."

"Your father's ignorance stops him from seeing that he needs this science far more than you do. Where do you currently live?"

"Monday to Friday, here. At weekends, I sleep at friends' houses or at the bus station; wherever I can find."

"Why did you not tell me this sooner?"

"You told me only to speak when it was absolutely necessary and it's only now that you have asked about my father."

"From now on, you'll stay here."

"Pai Nidê, will my stay here put you out? Won't it bother you?"

"Yes, more than you can imagine and more than you will be able to understand. However, it would bother me far more if you didn't come to live here."

With every day that passed, Iaô and Nidê grew closer. She thought the world of him. He became her everything: her God, her main Orisha. At the end of the celebrations, she sang his praises to the Heavens; pure praise for her Orisha Keeper, for her loved father:

*Oquê, babá*
*Babá de Orixá*
*Oquê, babalaô*
*Babalaô é um Orixá.*

This is how Iaô lived. Every day was a new challenge, a new task to learn. The change was noticeable. She started to see how immature her father, 'Peter Pan' actually was and started to laugh at his childishness. Her opinion of him changed completely. She now knew that he was unbalanced and obsessed. He was a person who had many psychological problems, resulting from his lack of happiness. He hindered people's chances of not giving up the fight for something, like he himself had done.

Iaô now understood that her father had persecuted Turunga because she was weak. He mistreated her to get back at his parents, Turunga's grandparents, who loved their granddaughter. He persecuted Mel because she was young, revolutionary and was fearless.

She was the polar opposite to him, a civil servant in Bahia's state bank. He traded his dreams for a fixed salary, which meant he had to work only six hours. He made up illnesses so that he could get permits. On the other hand, Mercinha had taken life by the horns, selling trust funds and costume jewellery, to pay her way.

Iaô understood the beatings that Mel had endured. It was a way of making her father feel better about his own, miserable life. He never hit Mercinha - not once! That would have been both revolutionary and daring. Had she never put him in his place? Yes, she had!

It was her mother's birthday and Mercinha had gone to visit her and give her costume jewellery as a present:

"And the pothead's arrived!" her father had called as she came through the door.

"Do you have anything to back up your claim? Hopefully, because I'm going to the police to tell them that you called me a pothead!"

"If you go to the police, I'll smash your face in!"

"Well then, you're going to have smash it in now, you coward! If you don't, it'll be me that's doing the smashing! Get up you drunken idiot! Who do you think you're talking to? You've already killed Turunga and Mel. Now you've got me, Mercinha, who's going to kill you! You're vermin! No, actually, you're worse! You make me sick! Don't you *ever* mess with me again! I'm not here because you're living in your own filth and you're stinking of God only knows what! I'm here to see my mother and brothers! Which reminds me, I've heard those lies you spread about me. The only drug that I ever used was when I was one of your sperm before conception! One of these days, everyone in this house is going to know what you are! Mother, I'm sorry for everything! I brought this gift and good luck!"

They were all in the living room. They looked paralysed. Mercinha was like this, born from Mel. She used to say to her friends:

"You used to know me as Mel; now you'll know me as Fel. Don't mess with me; you don't know me."

Mercinha was like this; she wasn't afraid of anything. She had friends in the slum. She knew 'thieves' and thought:

"These steal very little - a car... more often than not, parts of a car, or car stereos or the like. The real thieves are the ones that society applauds, puts in power, puts trust and faith in. I'm friends with the low level thieves. I'll leave the higher level ones for stupider people than me."

Iaô also understood Mercinha. She had discovered a lost legend in her screams and yells. She knew that her courage wasn't real. The lost legend that Iaô was now reading said:

"I can't bear any more pain. This awareness is what heightens my suffering. By hardening my heart, I feel less."

As a result of this, Mercinha cast away her spirit friends. She decided she no longer desired to live with her gift. She needed to exorcise her good side, in order to be able to live her life.

Iaô saw everything differently. She took something from each experience, and revelled in the satisfaction she achieved when she completed an arduous task.

She now lived in Nidê's house. There, she learnt to make dishes that could help balance, and strengthen, people's energy flows. Her friendship with Nidê grew stronger with every day that passed and, with every day that went by, they opened up more and more to each other. Iaô respected, and helped, Nidê and was sure of the good that Nidê was doing for her. Even when Nidê grew tired and short, Iaô understood.

Nidê didn't snap at her because of anything she had done, but rather was grouchy because of the exhaustion his old body felt. Whenever he shouted, Iaô took it to be Nidê's attempt to summon strength to be able to carry on working.

Like in martial arts, where the person shouts to find his, or her, primal strength, Nidê shouted to make his old, and weary, body come alive that little bit more, to enable him to keep working for that little bit longer. One day, hours after a ritual ceremony, Nidê charged Iaô with a task:

"Iaô, go to the São Joaquim market to buy some plastic cups."

This request seemed strange. It was a distance from Nidê's estate to where the São Joaquim market was being held; so far, in fact, that she would need to take two buses. There was also a supermarket not far from Nidê's house, so why was she being sent all the way to where this market was to buy some plastic cups?

Iaô tried to change his mind and suggested the supermarket...

"Are you going to go where I've asked or not?"

Iaô went up to her room to get changed into something more comfortable for the journey. She put on a pair of old jeans and made her way to the bus stop.

"The old man has lost it; he has to have. Sending me to the market all this way away rather than to the supermarket, just to buy some plastic cups...? Later, in the supermarket, if I find and buy some plastic cups... yes, this is what I'll do. I'll give it a bit of time, drink from a few coconuts down at the beach, in Itapuã, then head back to the estate. No, thinking better about it, I probably shouldn't. I'll just do what he asked."

So there Iaô went to buy plastic cups from the market in São Joaquim.

She searched high and low, but no joy. It was a Saturday afternoon and the *bombonière* that would normally sell cups like this had already closed. Iaô felt disheartened: "He isn't going to believe me if I say I was here. Either that or he's going to say that I didn't search properly. I know. I'll go to the supermarket and buy the cups from there. No, better not. Oh God, what should I do? I know - one of Pai Nidê's friends, Mr Ariosvaldo, has an estate a little bit further up the street from here, where he grows all those herbs and what-have-you. He has a phone. I'll give Pai Nidê a call."

"Good evening, Mr Ariosvaldo. Do you remember me?"

"How could I not! I was expecting you. I've already separated the herbs that Nidê requested yesterday. He called 'to enquire' as to whether you had arrived yet; he said you were on your way."

"What's that again?"

"Here are the herbs for the ritual this evening. He said for you to go straight back to the estate because you still need to prepare the *amaci* (bath of herbs)."

Iaô did as she was told. When she got back to the estate, Pai Nidê was already expecting her.

"I knew from the beginning you would come back with the herbs. By not just going to the local market, you passed the second test."

Pai Nidê and his tests...

* * *

At Nidê's house, work started early. Generally, Iaô was up and about before sunrise. She enjoyed trying to wake up before the sun.

"Pai Nidê, have you noticed that for the first few hours in the morning, the sky is at its cleanest and most visible?"

"How is that? I don't understand?"

"At night, you can't see the sky. We look at the moon, the stars and clouds. When the sun is strong, its light prevents us from looking at, and examining, the sky. In the first few hours after day-break, this is when we can see the blue becoming clearer in the day's first light. There are so many shades of blue, yellow, green and orange that are cast across the sky as the sun comes up."

"What I'm wondering, Iaô, is where your way of thinking, and talking, comes from? I honestly have no idea. What I do know, however, is that you need to find a way to express these thoughts. If you don't, you'll become someone who is sad, nostalgic and bucolic. What do your spiritual mentors say about all this?"

It was rare for Nidê to ask me anything about my spiritual mentors. He continued:

"I understand about energies from nature and the Orishas. I know that our ancestors exist; people who, whilst they were alive, developed a simple, balanced life with the elements found in nature and with the people around them. I also know that the ancestors never died; that their spirits inhabit space in the spiritual world and, there, they continue to work to maintain balance, peace and light in the world. Despite this knowledge, I don't know where they go; I never see them. In our work, Iaô, I'm going to be responsible for your energies and your Orishas. I believe that, if your Orishas are aligned with your balanced energy, if these spirits you call mentors willed you harm, then your natural energy flow would reject them and send them away. We'll put this to Tempo, an Orisha who de-cides the fate of those things in life that are harmful and that cannot be made eternal."

Whenever Nidê asked about Iaô's spirit mentors, it was be-cause it was important. He was now interested in finding out what the mentors, or ancestors, thought about her tendency to look so closely at the clouds in the sky. Iaô replied by simply stating that the topic had never been discussed:

"When I next see them, I'll ask."

"Child, sit here. Let's make this quite clear. I need to know how you see and hear them. Don't rush and don't be afraid."

"Well, first I feel their presence. It's like a chill on the nape of my neck. It's cold, a little alien almost. Everything that is around me becomes distant. Blemishes fade. My heart races. It's hard to explain how my skin, hearing and eyes all become more sensitive. My whole body becomes more aware. Amplified? I don't know if this is the word. When I feel these things, I know that my mentors, or ancestors as you call them, are coming close. They appear; they look into my eyes and touch my forehead with their pointing finger. I then become acutely aware of what they are saying and I see them clearly. Whilst we are talking, everything else around me feels so far away. They explain that my awareness in these moments penetrates the very fabric of the time and space they are in. I don't know what this is exactly. I still don't understand it completely, but they have said that, one day, I will understand."

"So what do they say to you?"

"They tell me everything and, at the same time, they tell me nothing."

"There you go again with your cryptic answers."

"Now it's my turn to not understand, Pai Nidê."

"I've been watching you for a long time. I have even discussed you with some friends in the Masonry. Some of them have even come here, to see how you work up close…"

"Who, Pai Nidê?"

"This I can't tell you. They have told me that you possess a language, a knowledge and an understanding of hermetic science."

"Pai Nidê, they're mistaken because I haven't the faintest idea what you're talking about."

"The ancestors that come to see you never told you about this?"

"No. We talk about my daily jobs and about those things that I struggle to accomplish. We have already spoken about time. They want to show me that death doesn't actually exist. They tell me about transformation, transmutation and the differences that exist between the two processes. It's as I said, they tell me everything but, at the same time, they tell me nothing. We talk and we think; we think and we talk. It's good. I'm then left with something that I don't know how to decode."

"Do all the spirits you see look the same?"

"No. The spirits that are suffering, and those that are aggressive, are very different. I feel sick in the stomach; my head begins to hurt and I feel annoyance for no reason at all. My body trembles. It's a horrible feeling. Since I have come to your house I have felt better and my spirit friends have told me that I am stronger for it. Because my energies are balanced, then my energies don't connect with the pain, the suffering and the chaotic energies that these aggressive spirits feel within their own etheric bodies."

"Child, why haven't you told me all this?"

"You've never asked before. Whenever I try and tell you about my spirit friends, you always stop me mid flow."

"Do you know what I think? You know a great deal, but you are still trying to understand the importance of this knowledge. What do your spirit friends think about me?"

"They think you are a good man and that you are helping me greatly."

"Go and wash the Orisha's room."

"I already have done."

"Well then, go and pick some herbs for your bath."

"Again, I already have done."

"Well, go and find something to do. I need to be alone with my thoughts!"

Pai Nidê was like this... there were hours where he would open himself up and listen to me. Then there were hours where he would have none of it and would close himself off from the rest of the world, to think and reflect. He would then, later, consult his *búzios*, a divination, using cowrie shells. Maybe looking for someone like minded with whom to share his internal certainties?...

Iaô adored Pai Nidê. She used to like to look at him. She was always impressed by his skill when he danced the sacred dances, as well as his understanding of the Orishas. She admired how he knew how to read, and perform, the specific movements within the dance:

"Orisha appeared and kept its left hand closed. Go, get a piece of paper and write something, Iaô. You need to write, draw, sew… It's necessary to do something with these hands of yours, to make sure that the energy keeps flowing correctly through your arms." He continued:

"Iaô, Orisha appeared with a hunch in its body, almost to the point that it was a hunchback. You need to take baths in herbs and meditate at night when it is a crescent moon. Tomorrow, we're going to go to the sea and you're going to bathe in its waters. This will help you."

And it did. Every day, Iaô transformed and transmutated. She transformed into a happier person, now aged 21.

Two years of intense work flew by. Iaô became an adult, but never lost her childlike spark. This harmonious transformation encouraged her energies to transmutate. Iaô changed back into Turunga. As one part of her grew older, another part regressed. She started feeling secure in herself again, as if her grandparents had taken her back under their wing. She took care of the animals on the estate, in much the same way as she had done when she played with her animal friends in the gardens of the houses she had lived in as a child.

"Iaô, grab me the big chicken so that we can poach it."

"Better not, Pai Nidê! It's not walking like it used to; I think it may be sick."

"Well then, get me the one that came from Angola; that chicken is almost ready."

"That one? But she's worse than the other. I tell you what; I'll go to the market and get us another one for dinner."

"What do you think is wrong with them, Iaô?"

"I don't know, Pai! We'll have to see if whatever is causing it comes from the water or the food they're having."

"There's nothing wrong with either the water or the food. The problem is that you care too much about them. Who do you think you are fooling? I'm going to stop rearing hens here. You care too much about them and I fear I'll get ill from eating them. You even go as far as to hide the eggs. Did you think I didn't know?"

"If we eat all the eggs, how will we get chicks?"

"Why would we want chicks? We're not going to talk about this anymore. I'm not going to eat your chickens. But from now on, you're going to pay the food bill. Go, get down to the market. It's already late."

So Iaô ran down to the market, feeling the same happiness that Turunga used to feel; a happiness that fought back and held Mercinha at bay, together with her pain, that would, from time to time, bubble to the surface. From Turunga, Iaô learnt happiness and confidence; from Macarrão, she learnt courage ; from Mel, determination and from Mercinha, the importance of not living life in ignorance.

With regards to her family, Mercinha knew one thing for certain: "I am, to them, like a slab of meat, a product that always needs to look good, be perfect and smell fresh. If ever once I didn't meet these standards, they would cast me aside." Mercinha always had to be praised and put on a pedestal, to be admired by everyone around her. She always had to be in the right and well-behaved, to be able to receive any attention; any love; any recognition. When she made a mistake, nobody offered her guidance to show her how to improve; rather they abandoned her and wanted nothing more to do with her.

If ever anyone said anything bad about Mercinha, no-one ever came to hear her side of events. As time went by, my soul came to realise one thing: for whatever reason, they don't want me near them. Perhaps it's because I bring back bad memories of fights and upset. Perhaps it's because I'm different. To be honest, I don't know the reason. Over time, I grew weary of trying to show them my good side. I was tired. I couldn't do right for doing wrong. It was impossible to make everyone happy all of the time.

Nowadays, I live with people who know about the skeletons I've got hidden away. They exchanged abandonment for my being in their lives and for helping me develop and evolve. They are people with whom I am able to share my best moments and who like what I have to give.

In talking about different parts, Halu Gamashi emerged and accompanied Iaô in her happy journey to the market. Halu Gamashi watches Iaô in her memories as she made her way down to the market to buy a chicken for dinner. Iaô, now, is a hero to her two chickens. Iaô, now, is the enemy to an unknown chicken that was going to die so that her two back at the estate could live. Halu Gamashi recalls Iaô's 'villainy' and how the unknown chicken was traded for money in the market and then tossed into a sack.

Iaô and the unknown chicken returned to the estate, where the chicken was soon devoured. Oh, how good it tasted! The two chickens that were spared continued to live long lives, under the protection of their heroine, Iaô.

* * *

"Iaô, when you have finished cleaning the Orishas' rooms, go and sit a while at the base of the Tempo's tree. Close your eyes and try to clear your mind. If you can't, watch yourself clean Oxalá's room over and over again."

"Pai Nidê, I've been wanting to ask you something for a long time!"

"As long as it is just the one…"

"Why do we need to clean the Orishas' rooms every day? They are always so clean and still smell of the cleaning products from the day before…"

"Is this a question or a complaint?"

"Definitely a question - it's the job that I enjoy doing most!"

"Really? And why is that?"

"The smell of the special herbs for the baths, the lights and the way I feel when I'm in there."

"What do you feel?"

"Each Orisha is different: in Ogum's room, my legs feel stronger; I clean that room the fastest. In Oxalá's, I feel tired; just smelling the herbs makes me drowsy; it just hits me."

"The next time you feel tired when you're cleaning the room, grab your mat and get some rest. Now, go and finish the jobs I've given you."

"Pai Nidê, forgive me but you didn't answer my question."

"What question?"

"Why do the Orishas' rooms need to be cleaned every day?"

"You don't clean their rooms. The rooms clean you. Once you've been cleansed by them, you are able to draw in the energies in the room more easily. The sensations you have just told me about are manifestations of the Orishas' energies."

If you ask questions, you want answers. Turunga was always asking questions. Mel and Mercinha, despite their life experiences, didn't lose this ability, which was passed on from Turunga. Now, Iaô is able to enjoy this talent also and, as a reward, is able to hear the answers that will help her understand her gift.

Asking questions and querying everything is something genuine in me. By understanding the world and social circle, I was later able to come to the conclusion that everything encourages us to muzzle the soul. At the moment, Halu Gamashi, who has also not been muzzled, has emerged into and shares the same space as Iaô. In Halu Gamashi's opinion, the best lesson Iaô learnt was to distinguish between things that are superficial and the things that matter.

The Roman Catholic and Apostolic Church was, for a long time, the official and traditional religion that was socio-economically accepted throughout my country. It survived and conquered the hegemony by creating stereotypes. It specialised in this; in particular, in distorting and deceiving reality, with the aim of distancing people from the things that matter.

This entity reduced to stereotype the basis of any religions and sciences that didn't share its aims and proselytisms. People took as basis the stereotypes it created and, from there, distanced themselves from deepening into other religions and sciences that were not 'catholically' similar.

In order to not be associated with stereotypes, people took refuge at the Roman Catholic and Apostolic Church. One example of antimagnetism is:

"I'm launching a harmful campaign about everything and anything. The only thing that will remain will be my religion and the doors to the Church will always be open."

African culture didn't escape this inquisitor action. In my opinion, African culture was the most persecuted, yet also the strongest, given that it fought back and didn't succumb, as other sciences and religions had done, before Catholic reactionary thinking.

Black Africa, including the groundwork and settlements, along with its kola nuts, the *obis* and *orobôs*, were stronger. The herbs used in the rituals won out! Africa kept its alchemical secrets hidden in silence.

Halu Gamashi, thinking back on the lessons learnt by Iaô, saw how rich and competent the content of Afro-Brazilian science was.

Whilst Halu Gamashi also knew how much there was a lack of character, the need for projection dilapidated the image of these sacred learnings. Many scholars, and fans, of Afro-Brazilian sect science/religion finished collaborating with the Catholic Church without even noticing, as they would desecrate it and use the teachings for purposes other than those for which they were intended, but without sufficient knowledge to realise what they were doing.

I'm saying this so that it is perfectly clear; I'm not apologising, or launching a campaign, and I'm especially not recommending any particular religious house, or Candomblé, or Umbanda Centre. My knowledge in this field has been obtained from people who have disassociated themselves from what we see all around us in our daily lives.

I'm not a stereotype, nor am I judging or classifying things. I am telling my story, and describing the experiences I have had, with people I have met along the way.

Insight is the first quality that a traveller must have. Travellers will move around, without understanding where they are going or where they are, until they develop discernment.

Iaô had a great deal of insight; Mr Humberto even more so. His perception was due to the people he introduced to her; hers was for having accepted, and taken advantage of, the wealth of knowledge found in Afro-Brazilian sciences.

The time has now come for Iaô to say goodbye. I cannot talk about her death, as she didn't die. She simply didn't want to. She remains alive until now, as she shares her life with Halu Gamashi. She has turned herself into a source, of sorts, that keeps the memories of Turunga, Mel and Mercinha alive. As a result of this, Halu will never forget where she has come from, the roads she has taken, the suffering she has endured and what she has learnt, despite often being surrounded by a lack of understanding and ignorance.

Turunga, Mel and Mercinha are all different experiences that make it hard for Halu Gamashi to reject people because of their stereotype. Because of her past, which has been damaged by prejudice and ignorant mentalities that permeate her experiences, Halu Gamashi feels compelled to throw herself wholeheartedly into the life, and soul, of those people with whom she lives.

On the other hand, this journey has made it so that Halu Gamashi does not become lost when she finds herself on the wrong path of false spiritual campaigns that are coursing throughout the world, and which make it difficult for the human race to become that little bit more human.

Iaô was born from a fountain, containing sweet Oxum water, in Pai Nidê's estate. Iaô was born from the fountain and preserved in its waters the memories of Turunga, Mel, Macarrão and Mercinha.

When something causes the waters filled with emotions to ripple, Halu Gamashi looks around her, to the sky and to the ground, in search of who or what caused the waters to be disturbed.

When something happens to make my emotions change I know that there is something, or someone, similar to the way I was causing the change. I need to stay on my path. I need to make sure I don't give up my lack of prejudice. I don't need to forget everything I have gone through by having avoided stigmas that have been corroded by pains, or which hide and suffocate the things that really matter.

Currently, I am Halu Gamashi. I don't know the name by which I will go when I die but, for as long as I am Halu Gamashi, I will not show prejudice towards those people I meet for, if I do, Turunga, Mel, Macarrão and Mercinha will have lived, and died, in vain.

# Second Part

# Introduction

What are we made of? There are many theories surrounding this question. I wonder? ...

• "Man is the result of his environment."

• "Traumas, fears, conquests, victories, losses and winnings are all the pillars upon which the human condition is built."

• "Genetics. Genetic inheritance is what humans are made of."

• "Man is made by what he sees, perceives and assimilates."

I'm not here to discuss philosophies and give thoughts on the study of human nature. But what is the concept of nature? Family? School? Society?

Life has led me to believe that Man can be looked at from a number of different perspectives. However, a 'person' is much more than 'Man'.

When we talk about 'Man', we talk about something impersonal and descriptive. When we talk about a 'person', this is more intimate and makes use of different emotions; as a sonnet, a prose, a Cabalist text, or something similar to old documents written in dead tongues, the type that are found by archaeologists in a cave hidden somewhere in the eastern continents.

It is filled with synonyms and antonyms and an endless number of genres. It even has something to do with the sympathetic and parasympathetic nervous systems, not to mention the skin... The skin is vital! Through our skin, we are almost able to 'touch our feelings' before we even name them, we are able to tell if there is 'chemistry' or not; whether or not we hit it off.

It makes you wonder... how easy could life be if we were all treated equally? The idea of equality is incorporated into every treaty that we, as humans, have written in history but, at the same time, is an abstract concept that is impossible to put 100% into practice.

'A person' has a name. 'Mankind' has a number.

Writing a bibliography at the age of 40 may seem ridiculous, according to some interpretations. Talking of interpretations... I believe that we are what we are, but that this is subjective depending on the person who is forming the judgement of what we are.

So here's how I would describe my rationale: person = interpretation.

I decided to write this book at the age of 40 because, up until now, I have never thought it necessary to put all this down on paper. I didn't want to leave off writing it until 60 because, to be honest, I don't know if I'm going to make it to that age. The bottom line is that I have a story to tell.

I have already told it a few times to a number of different people, but I have never put it down in writing, let alone in a book. The people I have told my story to have, of their own accord, decided to tell other people about me also. It is for this reason that I have decided to increase the number of people who know my story and the happenings that have occurred throughout my life.

Hearing people talk about me was the greatest thing that I learnt to deal with. The feelings, and sensations, that we have when we hear someone talking about their interpretations of what a person is (or isn't) can be comical, tragicomic, sad, painful, comforting and frightening; after all, humans are a combination of all of these emotions. This is completely different to what we would feel when we hear someone talking about our interpretations of what 'mankind' is or isn't.

I admit that it was from listening to what people have to say about me, and my way of living, that I decided to write my story.

The photos that have been included in this book were taken, over the course of a number of years, by different people.

The first time that my chakras opened, I was 25 years old. I was afraid and didn't have the faintest idea what was happening. I knew that it was an extension of my spiritual abilities, but how was I to live alongside this? What was I supposed to do?

Over the rest of this book, I'll talk more about this. I'd like to ask those people who are reading my book to read it to the end, but I give you fair warning, I am unable to tell you my entire story. The reason for this is that the entirety of a real person does not exist. If it did, you would not be able to fit everything there is to know about the person in just one book, or in just one mind, or just one space.

With all the baggage that we each have to carry, who is capable of finding space in their own body to fit another person's entire life? Everything that is written in this book is what I have seen, felt and understood throughout the course of my own life. There are other versions: people who have witnessed what I have gone through, and those who have heard things about me through the grapevine, have all come to their own conclusions about me.

Surviving in the knowledge that there are people out there who have never known me, nor ever met me, yet who know so much about me was the greatest lesson that my soul had to learn as Halu Gamashi.

From this, I allowed the lesson to change me and make me, without doubt, a little better. It helps me understand that everything in life is simply an interpretation.

We are in the era of writing, which started more than six thousand years ago despite not everyone knowing how to write at the time. We are in the era of writing, despite not yet having pulled down the Tower of Babel. My books have started to be translated into other languages and it's amazing how difficult it is to tell the story of one who has lived in Brazil, in Bahia, to people who live in other countries, who do not understand Brazilian and Bahian culture and way of life.

We are in the era of writing, despite everything. I just wonder now if we have also reached the era of reading? I think that we are in the process of bridging the gap between the era of writing to the era of reading. It's more than a bridge, it's a toll-bridge. If we don't have values that are inherent to not judging those around us, and if we continue to judge people, then we don't pay the toll. We don't cross the bridge and we don't learn to read.

Do you know what this toll is? The toll for the bridge is interpretation and the bridge is context. It is important to be aware of this: what is written will be interpreted by whoever reads it. The way we interpret the text is like a code, or values, or intentions of the person who is reading it.

Trying to understand the context is very important if we want to be able to reach the era of reading.

In my books, I aim to contextualise my story so that the reader has all the necessary resources to be able to understand it. However, it is difficult to contextualise such an unusual story for other people.

One thing is for you to contextualise the story of someone who is drinking water, driving a car, giving birth, going to a funeral or a celebration. Everyone knows what you are talking about, as we deal with these things on a daily basis.

It's something quite different to be able to contextualise the story of someone who has paranormal experiences and who was born in Bahia – a place of many religions and truths; in an unusual family, where the paternal grandfather is an atheist, the paternal grandmother is Catholic, the mother believed, and followed, any and all religions, and a father who believed Hitler to be the best person in history and Christ the worst.

Is that sufficient for contextualisation? I'm trying to help the reader understand how Turunga, Mel, Macarrão, Mercinha and Iaô all joined together to form Halu Gamashi.

# What can be said about the first time my chakras opened?

At the end of the 1980's, I left Pai Nidê's estate. I had been there for eight years. I'll tell you what happened:

Pai Nidê spent six months testing me, before taking me into his home to work with him, as an apprentice. During these six months, either consciously or unconsciously, I prepared myself for a new life, which was approaching slowly with every year that passed. I learnt, I improved, I grew… each year that went by, I deepened my knowledge of the four elements: fire, earth, water and air. I did this slowly, without any urgency, with no end date in sight.

In the beginning, I used to wonder:

"How long will I spend studying with you?"

"You'll stay here until you finish learning what you need to learn and also what you want to learn! Let's think about the quality of the time that we're together as, God alone knows, the length of time that we'll be together."

The passing of time was bringing me round to believing that we weren't going to be separated. In hindsight, I had so much to learn… afterwards, I stopped thinking about it and just allowed time to pass by.

Without any prior warning, life gave me the sign that meant I had to leave.

"Father, I've already washed the Orishas' rooms. Everything is covered in straw and white cloth, just like you suggested…"

"Good! The carnival celebrations are coming soon with all their heavy energies. We must protect our energies and keep them organized... Now, go and get your clothes, it's time for you to go."

"Go where, Pai Nidê?"

"Another chapter in your life has come to a close. You must now move forward into the next."

"I don't understand what you're telling me, nor will it work if you say that I'm deaf when I know that I'm not."

"That's just it! You're not anymore, but if you stay here that will change. You need to go out into the world and say what needs to be said."

"When should I come back?"

"Never! Never come back, child! Your life is different to mine. I'm a Babalorixa. Part of me was supposed to teach a part of you, and now it has. It's now time for you to do something with that knowledge."

"Why can't I do that here, with you?"

"Because you need to find your own way. Use what I have given you, together with what you already have inside you, and set out on your path. If it is meant to be, then you'll take pieces of what other people have to offer also. You will leave your mark on those people and, in doing so, will pass on what you have learnt from me. This will give birth to your spiritual energy flow. This is what we believe in our Orisha family."

"How does it work, Pai Nidê?"

"It's a sacred knowledge, child. Mankind across the world needs to have this knowledge; the Orishas are energies that Olorum freed from his sacred conscience. Olorum is the divine word that the African ancestors gave their one and only God. Depending on the people, the culture, the intelligence, the interest, the understanding and nuance of the word, they will take on one of God's faces. There is no-one, nor will there ever be anyone, who understands the Lord in his entirety.

"That's beautiful, Pai! Tell me more."

"The first wise men from Africa taught their disciples that the planet Earth, the *Arê* as they used to call it, is a special place, that Olorum chose for man to be born into, to grow in and to live in his image. For mankind to be born and recognise himself as part of an origin, Olorum agreed that they could be born from one another. This created the carnal family. For them to grow, Olorum sent them Orishas, who knew how to communicate with mankind. These Orishas became Parents, helpers to the humans. From there, the spiritual energy flow, as it is called by us, the Orisha family, was created. When the blacks came from Africa to Brazil, these helpers found them again, here in Bahia, and rejoined their spiritual energy flow."

"Are they only here in Bahia then, Pai?"

"No, child. But I do know the African family roots that made me join the spiritual energy flow are. You are also connected by these roots, now."

"Am I part of the family then?"

"Yes. You are my child. You will follow in my footsteps and will cause this energy to spread, and grow, by extending it to those people that Bessem, your Orisha, recognises as family also. Along the way, you will find people who will ask to be adopted into the family. If they connect with the essence of your energy, then they are permitted to join. If not, they will become ingrates. In other words, if they have already deviated from their original families, they are already ingrates. They will need to transmute this ingratitude to be able to take over the spiritual network with an energy that will reconnect them with Olorum's divine source."

"Am I an ingrate?"

"This is something that I would never think of saying. What I will say, however, is that you are at the point whereby you need to collect your things and set off on your own journey; to live your life as your conscience, and virtue, see fit. Your *raison-d' être* is not the same as mine."

I cried so much; I didn't know how to protest. What could I say if I, myself, had been dreaming of new paths, new journeys or new starts for the last few months…

This is pretty much the last time that I saw him. I looked for him so many times before he passed, in person and by phone, but he never responded.

"Tell her that this fondness isn't healthy, for her or for me."

I withdrew into myself. I cried. I understood and I accepted it.

I returned to my path. Eight months passed between the end of my time with Pai Nidê and the start of my new journey.

I left his home, carrying little but my own life. My life, back then, was everything that I had learnt from him. I took a few items of clothing; no money. Everything I owned fitted into my rucksack.

"It's better like this," I thought, "at least it's not heavy."

On the other hand, knowledge and experience weighed more on my shoulders. What was I supposed to do with all of this knowledge? Up until this point, I had known what to do with what I had learnt from Pai Nidê, having lived in his home and gone with him to see his patients and clients. Everything had made sense; everything had been certain.

"And now? What am I to do with my life?"

I found my family the same day. I was about to turn 27. My parents were living in a house in the countryside, in the state of Bahia. My brothers lived with my aunt in Salvador, as they were studying in the capital. My parents would often come to see them.

When there were long weekends, because of bank holidays, my parents and siblings would go to Cacha Pregos, on the island of Itaparica.

For as long as I can remember I, Halu, have always remembered Iaô, with her rucksack on her back, visiting them for the holidays on the island.

"Long time no see!"

"Sis, is everything ok? Have you just arrived?"

"Come in, I'm grilling some fish."

"What did she come here to do?"

My father was never ever amenable with me. If he were still talking to Mercinha, this visit would have, without doubt, ended in a fight. But he was speaking to Iaô. I, Halu Gamashi, think of the two of them and can remember that the person who responded to his question was Iaô:

"I came to visit you. What are you going to do at the Carnival?"

I was very calm. There's always great sadness whenever our emotions weigh heavy on us even though, paradoxically, we become subdued and it makes us calm. I believe that great calmness helps to dilute the sadness.

It was the first time that I had managed to spend an entire month with my family without killing each other and without me rising to my father's goading. I obtained work in Cacha Pregos, in a friend's restaurant:

"Mel, you're here?"

"I just arrived, today."

"How long are you here for?"

When faced with this question, Mel was able to allow her tears of sadness out. She told her friend that the future was uncertain.

"Well, whilst you're deciding what to do, come and help me in the restaurant. I need a cook. Can you also sing?"

Safe in the knowledge that she now had a steady job and set income, Iaô was able to live life a little more the way that Mel used to. She thought: "Pai Nidê said that, once a moment has passed, it's gone forever. I won't go back to being Mel."

When the holidays ended, my family went back to their normal lives. My brothers went back to studying, my father returned to work and my mother went back to the way she had been living, as the intermediary between my father and brothers.

After my family had gone back to their normal lives, I stayed on in Cacha Pregos for a further seven months. At the end of the summer season, my friend no longer needed me to stay on. I didn't move out of my parents' house on the beach. Instead, I took up fishing and started selling shellfish and crustaceans. This is what, in effect, kept the roof over my head during this period of my life.

Fishing meant silence, and silence meant reflection. As I reflected more, my life began to make more sense.

The pain of leaving Pai Nidê never really left me. Whenever people judge what they don't understand, when they disparage the world around them, when they disrupt the peace with their own preconceptions, this sadness returns.

I make the most of peace and thank God, Orishas and myself for having known, and having given myself to, the moulding hands of my dear friend, Nidê. He was a true, spiritual leader, who taught me not to accept lies that have been fabricated by lesser beings about what it is to be, or stop being, a spiritual leader.

I haven't given his true name, for the same reason that I haven't cited any other people by their actual names: this is, after all my story, about how I saw the world, how I lived and the way I interpreted what was around me.

I got through this difficult time. I left Cacha Pregos and moved back in with my aunt and brothers; back into the same house that I had run away from thirteen years prior.

To be able to earn my keep, I went back to selling insurance, this time working for myself, and started singing in bars again. As it wasn't a fixed income, I was only able to make enough to feed myself.

I didn't go looking for Mr Humberto. That inner voice always told me: "Leave the past in the past."

My spirit friend advised me:

"*Calm down. A new journey is about to start. You will experience great things. Don't be in a rush to try and understand and interpret them. Live what you need to live, just live it. Yes, you will have questions. Some you will vocalise, others you won't. There will be people who will pressure you into giving answers you don't have. Tell them that the answers cannot exist in the same time and space as haste. Over the next two years, you will live through so many things. You will learn about the Ether, the fifth essence, and this new knowledge will take you to new, unimaginable places.*"

When I heard this, something stirred inside me. I knew that something was going to happen; it was just a feeling I had. I was so focused on this feeling that I didn't even realise that it had already started to happen. The first indication of this was that I started having dreams.

I dreamt about people that I didn't know, people with whom I could talk for hours, and, when I woke up, I remembered each and every one of both the people and the speeches, with crystal clarity.

# Pictures - Chakras Opening

*1. Halu Gamashi dancing with Bessem, in the barracão, a large tent. It was the final moment of an energy alignment ritual, in the Keto nation.*

*2. Halu Gamashi presenting her Orisha, Bessem, in the barracão, during the Keto ritual.*

*3. Halu Gamashi with Bessem, asking to be blessed by the other Orishas and by Olorum.*

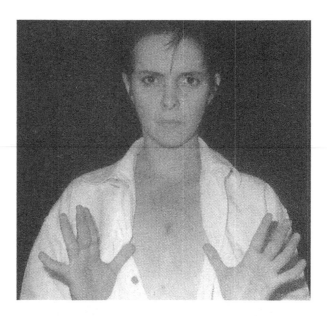

*4. Halu Gamashi, about 27, when the heart chakra (in the centre of her chest) opened for a second time and the upper synesthetic chakras opened (centre of her hands).*

*5. A side view of Halu Gamashi when the frontal chakra opened (the moment when scar developed).*

*6. Halu Gamashi when the frontal chakra began to open (side view).*

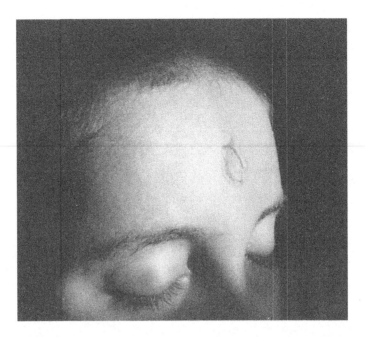

*7. The frontal chakra opened.*

*8. The frontal chakra opened.*

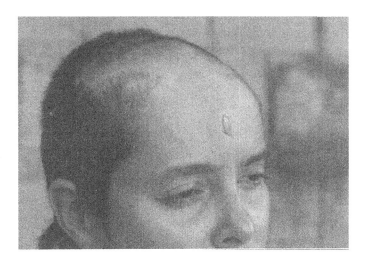

*9. The frontal chakra opened.*

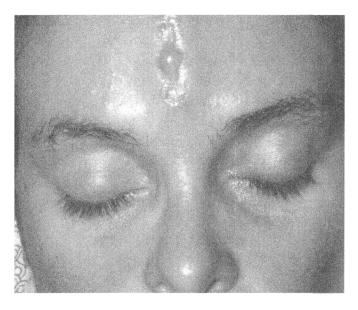

*10. Sequential stages of how the chakras opened for Halu Gamashi. This is the start.*

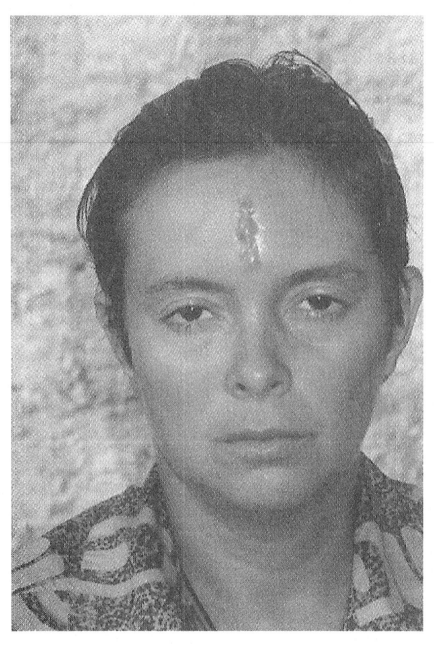

*11. The day after that on which photo 10 was taken.*

156 – Halu Gamashi

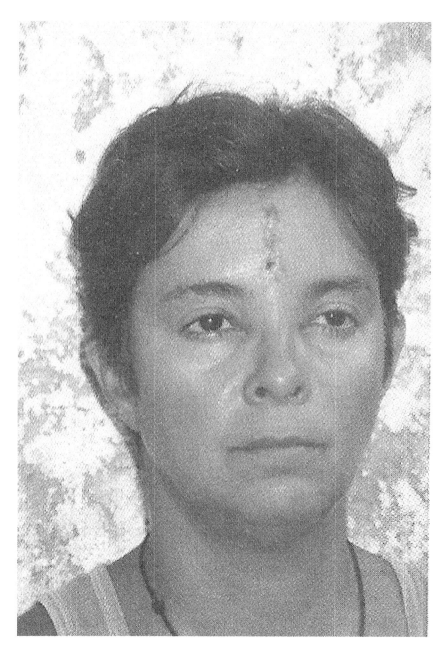

*12. Roughly a week after the start of the scarring stage.*

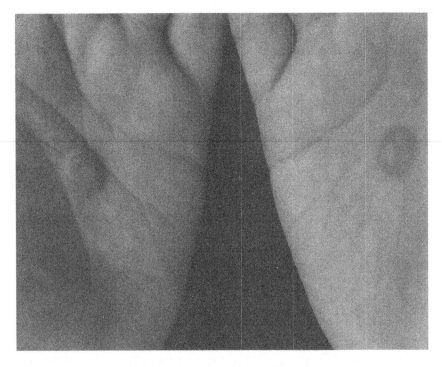

*13. Halu Gamashi when the upper synesthetic chakras opened (the blisters in the centre of her hands).*

"These dreams of yours are certainly different, Mel. They're like a novel, with a story line and everything." a very close friend, who I'd told about my dreams, said to me.

The second indication I noticed was that I started to sleep more than I otherwise had done. There were times I would sleep 24 hours a day and this happened on more than one occasion. My aunt began to grow scared of what was happening to me:

"I called you down for lunch yesterday and you didn't wake up. The same happened when I called you down for food in the evening. Are you taking sleeping tablets?!?"

"Of course not, auntie! I sleep and I dream, and I dream a lot."

I wasn't really feeling like talking to anyone else about it. There was nothing to explain. One day, my mother approached me:

"Do you think that you are suffering from depression? I read something about this once. Sometimes depression starts like this. People go into themselves and they don't want to leave their room."

"It's not depression, mother! I leave my room, I go out into the street, I go to work and I spend time with friends. I'm not depressed."

"Even so, it wouldn't hurt to see a doctor."

I went to the doctor to put her mind at rest, but the doctor was unable to find anything wrong with me. Sleeping for between 16 and 24 hours became less and less rare.

I would wake up after having had more long dreams, the majority of which had my spirit friend in them; others would have people I had never met in them. I gave nicknames to the people I didn't know, as they only appeared in my dreams.

I spent two months like this, until the day when I fell asleep outside and woke up with a blister in the centre of each hand. That was when I realised that my chakras had opened for the first time.

Going back to when I woke up that morning, I woke up slowly. I had had a powerful dream. In it, I was in a cave. Someone told me that, outside of the cave, people walked through the world with no knowledge of their own existence. I left the cave and saw these people walking, as if they were robots. I saw that they had a grey stripe, resembling cement, on their foreheads. Someone said to me that this stripe needed to be removed, so that people could see themselves again, to stop them hurting and suffering.

Back then, I didn't know anything about chakras. Some people I knew explained them to me.

I also asked my spirit friend to teach me about them.

"What are chakras? Is this what's happening to me?" I asked, innocently.

*"Don't let yourself be influenced by anyone. I told you that there were some spiritual experiences that you were going to have throughout your life. Do you remember? These experiences are happening to you now; don't rush them. It will all happen in good time. Embedded knowledge prevents wisdom from being expressed. People evolve and this is normal. They are surprising. Learn to live with this, but don't allow yourself to fight change."*

"Do you understand what you are asking of me? It's not easy

going through this and not having any explanation from you as to what is happening."

"*It would be even harder if I didn't let you come to your own conclusions. On the contrary, you would live your life the way I tell you to live it. This isn't how I work. It is important for you to learn to speak about what you are going through, by drawing upon your own understanding of it.*"

It took me some time to assimilate this new information. Two days after the blisters had appeared on my hand, I woke up in the early hours with an incredible pain in the middle of my forehead.

'Incredible pain' is a term that I better understand after what I felt. In fact, it wasn't pain as in toothache where the pain is short and burning. It wasn't like that. So how should I describe it? It was an indescribable, intense feeling. It was localised, profound, intermittent and almost unbearable.

It's difficult to find a term that explains what I felt, and so I settled with 'incredible pain'.

All of a sudden, this pain filled my head. It felt like my head was going to explode:

"It's going to explode! It's going to explode! My head is growing from the inside out. There is something moving, walking in my eyes." I remember myself screaming.

I couldn't stand the pain anymore, so passed out, if you can call it passing out… I fell into a deep, and instantaneous, sleep. At least, it felt like it was a deep sleep. When I woke up, in reality, only five minutes had passed by even though, for me, it had felt like hours had flown by. I can't explain it. There are things in life that we go through that we aren't able to put into words. I want to be true to myself, but words cannot begin to show what it was like.

When the synesthetic chakras opened in the palms of my hands, and then when my frontal one opened in my forehead, a gateway opened, through which I was able to see into myself and clap eyes on a higher consciousness. You can see in photos 5 to 12 how this happened.

How can I begin to describe this and put it into words? How can I make you, as the reader, understand what happened using words when it wasn't through words that this understanding came to me?

Let's try. Over the course of twenty days, the blisters in the centre of my hands, and on my forehead, scarred. For the first three days I didn't get out of bed. I would sleep and, when I woke up, would feel as if more hours had passed than had in reality. It seemed like I was in a different dimension, where time passed at a different speed.

In the second week, I had started to carry out various activities again, even though I had the blisters on my hands and body. Things were different now, despite everything continuing to be as it had been. However, on this occasion, the return, and sensation, felt far more powerful, more profound.

I became aware of cause and effect, and began to think about the consequences of my actions, words and gestures before I acted. This, ultimately, led me to err less. I'm not just talking about making poor moral judgements. My thoughts, my logic and my reason had all joined together in a far more harmonious structure.

To show you what I mean, I've designed a mandala that represents the way in which chakras work together when they are in harmony:

•**Cause:** is everything that motivates us. This can be anything from a small wish to a life ideal.

•**Action:** is an attitude that we choose to enable the materialisation of our cause.

•**Reaction:** is a mirror that gives us a concrete image, provided that the chosen action is, in fact, leading us down the path towards our intended cause.

•**Dharmatic reaction:** is an image that acts as a sign to show that we are on the right path, that we have a clear conscience and that the cause we are striving towards is en route to being achieved.

•**Karmatic reaction:** is an image that acts as a sign to show that we have strayed from the cause. We are then faced with different options: completely change the intended cause; move away from our dreams and move closer to sadness and frustration and have our conscience weigh down on us.

When the action is dharmatic, we follow a series of steps in the search for the cause. However, if the reaction is karmatic, it becomes necessary to completely interrupt the action and go back to square one. There aren't dharmatic shortcuts that we can take to reach peace.

•**Consequence:** is the *literal* materialisation of the cause. The dream or ideal that was at the causal source is now being made a reality before your eyes.

My path changed and became slower. My body aligned; a surge of energy passed through my spine and made my body become more erect. As I walked, I felt my feet push against the ground. It was harmonic, smooth friction; an intimate relationship between the sole of my foot and surface of the floor.

"Is it possible that I am more alive now than I was before?" I asked my spirit friend.

*"It is possible. Given that your awareness is more finely tuned to life, with everything you touch and connect to."* my friend responded, trying to quench my thirst for understanding.

I spent the following 20 days surrounded by sensations. When the blisters faded, they left circular scars behind.

I tried to go back to work selling insurance and singing in

bars, but couldn't bring myself to do it. I returned an hour later, vomiting and suffering from diarrhoea.

A month later, I experienced my heart chakra open, right in the centre of my chest (see figure 4). I relived the same pain I described in earlier pages, growing out of a sense of pity, compassion for everything and everyone. I saw beauty in everything and everyone:

"What type of rose is that?" I asked.

"A red rose" the spirits replied.

"Is it a common red rose?" I asked again, without believing what I had been told.

"It is. Why?"

"The red is different. So is the rose."

When my heart chakra opened, my view of the world changed. It wasn't the same world I had lived in before. Everything I thought of as attractive previously I now saw as beautiful and what I saw as evil now appeared grotesque.

This transformation also had a great impact on my relationships with people. What others believed to be of reasonable importance, I now felt to be life and death.

I felt pain course throughout my body whenever I saw walls erected around trees; whenever I saw flowers being picked; whenever I saw people snapping twigs as they spoke to one another, completely unaware of what they were destroying.

"Are you blind? You're destroying the planet."

"What? What are you talking about?"

"Look at the ground. Look at the leaves you stripped the tree of, and the branches you broke, whilst you were talking."

"This girl really is mad. What's it got to do with her? It's my brother's house. It's not hers." he said to the girl he was with, who had helped him destroy the tree.

"He needs to be careful. She has her eye on the house and uses this story about spiritual awareness to try and take it." piped up someone else.

This is just one example, among a thousand others, of how I lived and what I experienced during this period of my life.

# The birth of Halu

I need to start this chapter by confessing that I am choosing not to include names of people that have been present in this part of my life. I'm not doing this because I want to. My main reason for focusing the story on me is because of the respect that I have, and would like to express, for each of those people. I don't want to involve them in my personal interpretation of what has happened.

Some of them followed their own paths, which has meant that I have not seen them for some time. Do they take part of me with them? It's possible. What I took from them has made me stronger and has strengthened my decision to tell my story in the way that I am.

As I have already said, a story can be told in different ways. This is because we are not numbers. Only numbers can add up to figures that will not leave behind any remainders. However, even numbers, despite being so precise, can still leave remainders when divided. Depending on the remainder that we have after the division, we can either round up or down.

This is what I am doing. From everything that I have lived through, what cannot be incorporated into my story leaves behind a remainder. In this book, I have rounded all the painful remainders down, and all the feelings of nostalgia up, for a broader conscience.

Halu Gamashi came to be at the end of the book: *An Apprentice's Journey*.

Halu Gamashi came into this world normally and, as she led her not so conventional life, has searched for a way to sign that book. What is the author's name? Whilst searching for a name, it dawned on her that everything is given a name by someone, and that the name that is given depends upon the reasons, the person who names the object had, at the time the name was given.

Mércia Celeste Dias de Silva, this name…, if it can be called that, dates back to when names were given, and lost, through marriage. The nickname, Turunga, was created so that order and progress could be established, and so that this tradition could be hidden in the same way that a cloud hides the sun.

The nickname, Turunga, didn't survive past school. It wasn't an easy noun for the youngsters to say. So what was Turunga? An abbreviation of Teresa? No, my name isn't Teresa! Then there was the next nickname, Mel, which stayed with me through my teen years.

The nickname Mel didn't survive my running away with the fleet of lorries. In fact, this is where Macarrão was born. After all, this was a more fitting name for a teenager who was so slight.

That said, Macarrão didn't make it through the terror of the Estação da Luz:

"Here in the metro you'll stop being known as Macarrão, and instead will be Minhoca."

"Bida, for the love of God, stop giving me these nicknames!"

"Macarrão doesn't fit either! What did they call you before you left home?"

"It depends. Everyone back home has lots of nicknames. The one I liked most for me was Mel."

And so Mel was reborn in São Paulo. She had other nicknames during this stage of her life: *Baiana*, run-away, *Sertaneja*, but Mel was the most commonly used one.

Mercinha has been the nickname that's been given to me by my family, on and off, throughout my life.

"Forget my name. Forget it; you aren't my family! Never let anyone know you are associated with this family. Don't humiliate us anymore!" My father used to repeat this phrase on a regular basis, so that it would be drilled into me.

There I was, looking for a name by which to go when signing my book. I chose Halu Gamashi, as this was my spiritual name. It was given to me by my spirit friend and mentor. Whilst I sat there, pen in hand, thinking back over how my name has changed periodically over the years, my spirit friend whispered in my ear:

"*Write the book as Halu Gamashi, the name of your soul.*"

In my book, *An Apprentice's Journey*, I wrote this story and so shall not repeat myself here.

People have asked me what this name means. I never asked my mentor. Understanding a name means understanding so many things: meaning, rationale, interests and intentions, whether explicit or implicit. But I do know this; I've lived through so much that, now, I don't think about what names mean.

When my chakras opened, my understanding grew. I went through processes of intense regression and spontaneous progression. I'll explain what I mean:

It's like Einstein said, time is relative. This scientist explained time using maths and physics. So was he successful? For some, yes; but for the majority, he wasn't.

I learnt about time relativity from my spontaneous, and genuine, trips to the future and the past. This process helped me better understand the topics I study. I have no control of when it happens, nor do I have any idea when it will happen again.

It starts like this; everything in me slows down. My thought processes become slower. In these moments, I find it hard to think back and remember my home. Everything melts away and it becomes impossible to determine when I met people. All I know is that I have met them.

I need to lie down and close my eyes, until all thought fades away into nothingness. My head completely empties. Tranquillity and calmness are established in my emotional camp. I will be completely aware that my Self will be guided by a greater consciousness in me.

As such, I get to know my Higher Self. This is the best part of us. Our dharmic, luminous, spiritual, physical and special centre holds all our victories and allows us to evolve.

This psychic space isn't kept contained in time within our mental consciousness. In this space, all our soul's memories and different times on Earth are logged.

So, by accessing my Higher Self I am able to go back, or move forward, through time. I have spent anywhere from five minutes to entire weeks like this. All those who help me, see me speaking either a different language, or Portuguese with a strange accent, which is difficult to place.

The next thing I do is try to find out where I am, who they are and then I introduce myself. I then, suddenly, 'wake up' and I recall everything, as if it were a dream, one that had been ongoing. Remembering the hours, and days, that I have spent completely immersed in this state is like remembering a dream. The only difference is that the memory is sharp and clear.

Depending on the length of time that I take, and the knowledge I learn, it can take anywhere from a day to three months to return to 'normal'.

As a result, I am able to travel forward or backwards through time. From this experience, I have come to my own conclusions about how, and why, time is relative.

It's obvious, in knowing that this can happen at any point, that this ability isn't at my mercy nor is it done at my convenience; it scares me a little. There is not a specific time, or date, when it is likely to happen. This used to scare me greatly and made me live my life to the extreme, in the sense that I became completely dependent on all those who were around me. I only felt safe if they were around.

This dependency has led me to believe that only they would be able to be close and that only they knew what was best for me.

So many theories were developed about me:

"Dual-personality, an alter ego…"

"But how? During this time, she talks about concrete ideas and has knowledge of things that she didn't have beforehand. No, this doesn't fit the profile of someone with a dual-personality. So what is it?"

"I know! She's remembering her past lives."

"But this doesn't explain how Halu is able to move forward to the future. What about destiny? Is it already written, in tablets of stone, what will happen in a hundred years from now? Is it?"

"It's a spirit that takes her over!"

"But that also doesn't fit the profile. It's not possible for someone to have a spirit in them for three months. What else could it be?"

Halu Gamashi was listening. She was speechless. She had no idea what to say. She was never consulted, but this is how she had spent her life. Every group she came into contact with had an opinion about her.

It didn't matter that there was evidence to the contrary, which shot down so many of these theories. Those that thought her to be either mad, or schizophrenic, sought to be away from her, presumably so that they wouldn't see her knowledge proved right through the work that she was carrying out.

There were those that even wanted to make her a kind of Catholic Saint from the Middle Ages:

"She makes predictions that come to pass. Her chakras opened. They're known as chakras by eastern cultures, and Christians refer to it as the stigmata of Christ."

"That's it! She's been stigmatized by Christ! Doesn't she bleed from the parts of her body where she bears the marks?"

"She does! From time to time she bleeds heavily, less so at other times. Other times, she would just sweat from them."

"Really? But she enjoys dancing, smoking cigars and drinking wine! It seems all too normal!"

I, Halu, continued to listen… continued to feel… I already knew how difficult it was to fit into preconceptions… I wondered what I was going to have to do? Was I to abandon a normal life, as some of them wanted me to? Was I to found Ashrams, as others suggested? Create movements? Dress in Indian clothes? Burn incense?

I rationalised - if this was what I was supposed to do, why was I born in Bahia? Why did I have a normal side to me? If I do what they ask of me then I will be mocked, a clown. Everything I do is fluid, spontaneous, comes from deep inside and works its way out. What foundations are needed to create someone with clothes, and behaviours, that work the reverse, making their way in rather than out? I tried it, once. I even bought clothes that were recommended to me. I felt ridiculous, fake!

"Now, yes, you are amazing! It suits you so well!"

"People, what is it that you see that I don't? I'm distracted, disconnected."

"We see you. We see someone who is balanced and dressed in clothes that work well with the scars on your forehead and hands. They frame the scars, where the chakras opened, perfectly."

This didn't last long. I didn't pay any attention to them. It wasn't natural. When I spoke to my spiritual mentor, he said:

*"They are suggesting that you look the way they understand what you are. There is a profile into which everything fits. Medical professionals dress in white, as do spiritualists and leaders in the Afro-religion-sect-culture. This ex- emplifies the need that people have to fall into a specific category, or have a spe- cific label. These people are telling you to dress like this because they want you to look the part for the public role they believe you should be fulfilling. Continue to go through life doing what you think and believe to be right. As time goes by, they will understand that it isn't possible to force you to fit into a role that they want. People will like Halu for who she is. Others won't, and will go looking for someone else who meets with their expectations. This is the only way you will be able to better understand your purpose here on Earth. You'll find out what your raison d'être is when the time is right."*

I spent some time explaining this conversation to the group. It was almost as if they were deaf to my words:

"Ah, yes! I understand. But you really do suit these clothes. What difference does it make? You only need to create a public im- age so that people know who they are talking to."

"But who are they talking to?" I asked.

"With a prophet!"

"With a higher spirit!"

"With the reincarnation of someone very important. You need to stop smoking cigars. You need to give up your normal life, give up sex, stop letting normal people close. You let us deal with this. We will build a group around you. You will write your books. We will organise their launch, the editing of them, the talks, the courses."

"You want to invent someone who doesn't exist, and this doesn't interest me! I have a side to me that is normal, like everyone else does. It just wants to live and express itself. I also have a side to me that is not like everyone else. I have psychic abilities, my chakras have opened, and I am able to connect with the Akashic registers. I was born with the ability to see those who have passed away as if they were still alive; I study at astral institutions; I have a cosmic memory, but I am not a Saint. I don't want to create a new religion; this isn't my raison d'être! I need to find a way to share my knowledge with people about the subtle body, about holism, mankind's relationship with the four elements and with the fifth essence."

I never understood why I needed to become a public figure. The two sides to me exist harmoniously together. One never bothered the other, but nothing separated them. There is no conflict between them. On the contrary, in fact, they complement each other. My normal side makes me connect with people's daily lives. I am like them; I know what it feels like and understand their pain, their doubts and share their weaknesses. I know the less human side to humans because I, too, have that side to me. On the other hand, my other side helps me find ways to develop ideas and proposals that I need. With regards to other people, the most I can do is suggest that they experience the same as I have experienced.

With these words, I was able to bring an end to the discussions. Some left, others stayed to try and convince me otherwise.

Each time someone left, I became surer of myself and the courage of my convictions was strengthened. Do you know why? I'll explain; as I didn't accept their suggestions, and theories, they completely changed their idea about me. The prophet would then become mad, lost, led astray. Everything I did resulted in these people giving me another lecture.

I congratulate myself for not having followed their suggestions. I congratulate myself for having chosen my own path. Do you know the path that I chose? The two sides to me communicate each day. Whenever my light is able to outshine my shadows, I know that I am becoming a better person.

When my chakras opened for the first time, I had my first experience with the fifth-essence, the Ether.

When my friend, two months prior, warned me that something was going to happen, I never thought that it would be this, nor did I expect it to happen the way it did.

I never thought that this blister in the middle of my forehead, that those in the palms of my hands, that the dreams and the rapid weight loss, were all associated with the early warning given by my spiritual mentor.

The fact is that the changes continued to take place and the chakras continued to open. My interest in the world changed, my values changed. A new consciousness took over my expectations and all my desires were left behind.

Before my chakras opened, I wanted to be a singer. I wanted to make a record, well, more than one really. I also wanted to become a philosopher. I liked, and continued to like, and believe that I will always enjoy philosophy. During the period in my life I'm referring to philosophy, for me, was understanding mankind in his human and inhuman life. I loved debating this topic with my friends.

My grandfather was responsible for this. As he was an atheist, he tried to understand my spiritual side using philosophy.

He passed down to me his enjoyment of studying philosophy and his thoughts on mythology, maths and, finally, all the educative branches of philosophy, all of which he introduced me to as a young child.

As I said, my values changed. I delved into topics relating to the paranormal, and spirituality, among other subjects. The most difficult thing, during this period, was connecting with people who knew me. They did not understand what was happening. Those that did know what was going on couldn't accept my transformation and evolution; they simply wanted Mel, forever. Then there were those, more radical, friends who wanted the rebel, Mercinha, back.

It was a busy time. The first few months of this new era in my life flew by. The speed with which time went by was directly proportional to the speed with which I was changing.

Over the course of two years, my chakras opened time and time again. They would scar me, before opening once again and, with each opening, I underwent an internal transformation, until I finally became who I am today, Halu Gamashi.

After much persuasion, I agreed to register the opening of my chakras by taking photos of them each time. That said, I don't have all of the photos from this time. Perhaps someone else has them;

maybe they're lost, who knows. As I wasn't interested in taking these photos, I never really paid much attention to how many were taken, where they went or anything else of that nature.

When my chakras opened, I gained the ability to travel, through sleep, to immaterial planes. Through this, I got to know the spiritual world and astral institutions.

It was a period during which I discovered a great deal and underwent a great number of transformations. As the months went by, those things that my spiritual mentor had foreseen came to pass. I wanted answers. The people around me wanted more than answers. They wanted explanations based on facts, which would correspond to their ideas. More than ever, I noticed how people are unwilling to gain practical experience. They were content with just reading the theory side of things in books, though I suppose that it is sufficient to read a book if you only want to have theoretical knowledge. Gaining practical knowledge takes time, patience, neutrality, lack of judgement, lack of pre-conceptions and reluctance to jump to conclusions.

The people around me didn't understand any of this. They learnt from books. I admit that I felt like a book, many times, when I was around them.

"What's this?"

"A chakra opening." I would respond.

"Why does it open?"

"I'm still not sure."

"How does it open?"

"I feel my body become slow, followed by an intense pain in the part of the body where the chakra is opening. Minutes later, that same part of my body will become very hot, then very cold. When it goes cold, the cold still burns. It's a 'heat' that comes from the bitter cold. A blister develops and the pain subsides."

"I feel tired and go to sleep. What happens after is difficult to explain. Knowledge opens and I internalise it instantly."

"But why does this happen to you?"

"I don't know how to give you a definitive response; all I can do is share my experiences."

"Did your spirit friend not tell you why this happens?"

"He just told me that there are many things to be said and dis-covered. I need to prepare myself for what is to come and this will take time."

"How much time?"

People and their haste. It was no use asking for them to be patient, even less so to ask them to remember to be so, for I wasn't a phenomenon, or something curious to satisfy their egos. These first years were very meaningful. My sensitivity was heightened greatly. It wasn't easy living with people rushing me for answers to satisfy their curiosity.

From the first few conversations with my spirit friend, after my chakras opened, I understood that my work was directly linked with energy that can be used to cure. This energy is a deepening of the knowledge that the subtle body has. Normally, what we refer to when we talk about cures is the recuperation of health. This curing energy is the alignment of energy that structures, and establishes us, so that we are able to live and co-exist in this world.

Sickness is clear proof that we are not structured and have not adapted to the four elements, or with what comes from them. Allow me to make a few references here: organic ethics, emotional ethics, rational ethics, egoical ethics and other laws that govern life.

When we say that, for every action, there is a reaction this is true. The girl that burnt the leaves and tree branches made a mistake because of my interference, because she was unaware that every ac-tion has a reaction.

When we get to know the subtle body, we learn to cure our imbalances from the inside outwards, whether they are physical ail-ments, or emotional, or spiritual ones.

Knowledge of how to cure the subtle body encourages us to organise our root, so that we are able to harmoniously feed our-selves and, from there, end the sickness, the weakness and a life in vain. I won't go any deeper into this topic for this isn't possible now. Anyone who wants to understand more about how my chakras opened, and discoveries I have made, will find they are all detailed in my book: *An Apprentice's Journey*.

After these first two years, I had experienced profound con-tact with the Light, with the Astral Institutes and with a higher spirituality. During this period, I learnt that the main chakras are located in the upper part of the body, from the coccyx upwards:

**Main Chakras**

•Crown chakra: located in the pineal gland region.

•Brow chakra (a.k.a: third eye chakra): is located on the forehead, between the eyes, and is associated with the hypothalamus.

•Throat chakra: located in the throat and associated with the pituitary gland.

•Heart chakra: located in the chest and associated with the thymus glands.

•Solar plexus chakra: found in the centre of the chest and is connected with the pancreas.

•Sacral chakra: located below the navel, between the coccyx and the knee.

•Root chakra: located between the knee and the perineum and associated with the genitals and sexuality.

**Secondary Chakras:**

•Upper Synesthetic chakras: located in the upper part of the phalanx of the fingers. The point of convergence is the centre of the palms.

•Lower Synesthetic chakras: located on the underside of the phalanx of the toes. The point of convergence is the centre of the feet.

**Tertiary Chakras:**

•All the pores of the body.

I am, currently, 42 years old. Fourteen years have passed by since my first experience. Up until now, my chakras have opened on a yearly basis. That said, I can't guarantee that this will carry on every year in the future.

Every time my chakras open, I experience things that cause my sensory organs to become heightened. I have now become able to see people's auras with more clarity. My hearing is also more acute, as are my senses of touch, smell and taste. Everything in me is different, as are the sensations that I experience.

The people that I surround myself with on a daily basis know, and understand, my heightened awareness. To describe it in just one or two paragraphs is, without doubt, an impossible task.

Whilst, in the beginning, I resisted including photographs of my experiences, today I see I was just being immature. Looking at the photos, I believe that the images contained in them can help me give the reader context of my experience.

There are so many things to talk about, to share, but I'm not in a rush. If one book wasn't sufficient, then I'll write others to tell the story. For those of you who are in a rush, I'll say that knowledge, and haste, do not share the same space.

# Five years later

I've said all I can, for now, about when my chakras first opened.

Five years after this first experience I was a very different person. I finished writing *An Apprentice's Journey* in 1995. Between 1990 and 1995, I lived in Salvador (Bahia), Belo Horizonte (Minas Gerais) and São José dos Campos (São Paulo). During this time, I gave lectures, seminars and courses about the spiritual world and about what I knew with regards to chakras.

I made many friends, and work colleagues, who remain with me even to this day. I left behind all those people who had no desire to know about the existence of a knowledge, which they are choosing to ignore completely.

There are people out there who cannot accept they don't know everything. When they come across an unknown topic, they distance themselves, and seek to destroy that which makes them feel uneasy. As I'm not writing a book about other people, I will bring the story back to me and my experiences.

In the beginning, everything is a novelty and, for me, this novelty alternated between enjoying the show and not understanding what was going on. I tried to get closer to the scholars, including people with letters after their name, who focused on studying the human psyche. As a result of my irreverence, once I met these groups, I started to call them 'alphabet soup'.

Normal people, who are in search of the true meaning of holism, spirituality, subtle bodies and the way in which all these work together in modern man, were those that supported me most.

It seems the so called 'wise' men are no longer open to new experiences. They stick to the old ways that they build up and place importance on their own egos.

This period was between 1990 and 1995. I call it the 'Era of Passion'. One of the projects from this time was to align myself with my friend, Reinaldo, to buy a Kombi, similar to those that are used for advertising in the streets. I dreamed of going out there and talking to anyone who would listen:

"The spiritual world exists! We are already born with the ability to achieve immortality. To do this, we need to know about chakras."

Even today, I want to share my experiences, and knowledge, with everyone around me. Life doesn't end. It just continues in a new way, with new goals, and I can testify that time is continuous. Space has many dimensions and the energy that forms dense matter is the same as that which forms subtle matter.

The flame that keeps us alive is ever changing. The changes it undergoes depend on a number of factors, including: karma, dharma, chakras and how we live our lives.

These factors are completely independent of each other and so it is impossible to give a definitive time when someone will incarnate.

The flame I'm referring to has nine stages of change. These changes take place at the same time as hormonal, anatomical, dental, intellectual and sexual changes:

**Table showing the stages of change:**
- 0 – 9 months (before birth)
- 0 – 9 months (after birth)
- 9 months – 3 years
- 3 – 9 years
- 9 – 18 years
- 18 – 36 years
- 36 – 72 years
- 72 years onwards
- 0 – 9 months (the stage when we return to the spirit world)

The life flame is the spark that keeps us conscious. From the moment that we gain consciousness, we are alive and we will never die. There is no point in us worrying about death. It's not going to happen. All we need to do is understand the way in which the flame changes.

From the moment that barriers between consciousness and unconsciousness crumble, our rational, and mental, consciousness increases. I acquired this when my chakras opened. For this reason, I am happy to testify: death does not exist! What is dead, or is yet to be born, is the study of our soul and its atemporality.

From looking at the table on the previous page, we can see that there are stages that repeat themselves. When they end one cycle, they start the next. These are the ages in which the changes to the life flame take place, as well as the emotional, intellectual, dental, sexual and hormonal changes.

To put it simply, we'll call them cycle-limits. During these stages, our mind changes our expectations, what we deem important, external interests and, at the same time, our life flame goes through its changes.

If we don't know about the chakras and the subtle body, we are unable to develop the necessary knowledge to be able to undergo these changes. For this reason, a large amount of our existence is 'lost' in the depths of our memory. We remember hardly anything about when we were little, in the first few years of life. We lose these memories when our second set of teeth start to erupt.

My dear reader; I sure don't expect you to deeply understand what I am saying. Whilst I write books, I am aware that, in order to pass on this detailed knowledge, it will take more than my goodwill, a book and a quick read. But, for now, putting a few words in writing is the closest that I, personally, can get to introducing the subject. Furthermore, apart from my desire to share all this with you, I cannot deviate from the main point of this book.

In continuing with my testimonies, I can also confirm that the energy that built the material world, the material body, is the same energy that built the subtle bodies and the spirit world.

What makes these two worlds different is the weight, the mass, the volume and the speed. These differences, naturally, are affected by gravity.

Now, I have to return to my story.

The 'Era of Passion' ended when I saw that I was going to need far more than just a loud speaker and a Kombi. It was going to be a long journey to be able to make myself heard. I had to take over a neutral space.

Everyone who heard me compared me to someone that they already knew. You have no idea how hard it is to talk to someone who thinks they know everything already. Without doubt, these first five years were the most difficult of my life.

Halu Gamashi remembers, in the 'Era of Passion', the pains that Mercinha felt, the knock-backs that life had given her, and how she bounced back each time with more conviction:

"During that period of my life, I didn't know what pain was."

Pain isn't being beaten by your father for not agreeing with his choices. Pain is being given orders through judging eyes that do everything to try and block each decision you make.

Pain is surviving a crime without being brazen about it. It is being surrounded by people whose lips recite hypocritical tributes and whose thoughts are aimed at you, petty and self-indulgent.

It is necessary to be strong and have the courage of your convictions in order to survive with such awareness. I believe that people may become individualist, egotistical, 'crusty crabs', as we say in Bahia, to stop themselves from understanding what this awareness can offer.

This was the difficult side to my experiences in the first few years after the chakras opened. Naturally, there were other painful experiences but, without doubt, living alongside hypocrisy is, even today, one of the hardest things that I have done.

In these first five years, I couldn't bear my body coming into contact with any synthetic material. All my clothes were made of cotton, not always the soft kind, sometimes the rougher type that is used to make dishcloths.

Being well-dressed in Belo Horizonte, the fashion capital, is all the rage though, back when all this was taking place, the clothes made with this type of fabric were not at all fashionable. When I went into a bank, a shop or someone's house, I would always attract attention.

I would fashion a beret. I still wear them now. At the age of 42 you can dress how you want. At the age of 40 we are emancipated, or at least I gained emancipation during this time.

Nowadays, I don't worry nor do I think about, or even associate myself with, people who judge people based on their first impression. Living with this torturing judgement from the silenced mouths of hypocrites, together with their 'burning glares' that cut and scorched my flesh, all formed part of my learning during the first five years of my journey.

As my tactile awareness grew, whenever I entered into an atmosphere where there was conflict, fighting, arguments, overindulgence of alcohol or even sickness, my skin would burn. This isn't a euphemism, a metaphor even less so. My skin actually burnt. It became necessary for me to seek medical attention for the burns, but this was nothing in comparison to the lack of understanding. In the event the 'landlord' found out about my burns:

"You burnt yourself like this in my house? Are the energies in **my house** that bad?"

I never sought to clarify. He would just stand there, silently. Why are the hypocrites not able to express their fear and cowardice using a reasonable tone when in public.

When these episodes took place in relatives' houses, or in the houses of friends of people that were living with me, the pain was greater. It only dissipated when I was alone.

"You're exaggerating; I've never heard anyone say a bad word to you. Your problem is that you want everyone to understand your hypersensitivity."

"But if they don't understand my hypersensitivity, how am I supposed to live with them?"

All questions without answers.

However, if these episodes happened in the homes of, or with people that were not directly linked through blood to, the people with whom I lived:

"Only they would be able to really burn you. What arrogant people!"

It was futile to explain that it wasn't exactly like this.

I have spent a great deal of time differentiating between belief and arrogance. Now, I know that there are people who behave arrogantly, and others who bring their beliefs. Acting arrogantly and acting according to your beliefs are opposite behaviours, which cannot exist in the same place. If we allow ourselves to behave arrogantly, we may never develop a concrete belief.

Yet, in the 'Era of Passion', Halu Gamashi didn't know how to differentiate between the two.

On the other hand, by being so acutely aware, she was able to have fantastic experiences. Being able to confirm that eternity exists is a real gift. Believing that time is relative, that space has many dimensions and that we live forever is a privilege.

This was my first big win, my real prize. Whilst I am able to share my story with people, it's not for me to develop their beliefs. This lifts a huge weight off my shoulders. When I realised that it wasn't my *raison d'être* to prove my beliefs to people, the 'Era of Passion' ended. Halu Gamashi had won what she called the 'Era of Matured Love'.

Whilst passion is hot, like the sun at midday, love is blinding and is mourned like the setting sun at the end of the day.

After my heart chakra had opened as many times as it had, I burnt my passions and started to discover what love really was. I passed through the gateway of compassion, for everything and everyone, and into the atmosphere of love. Compassion is a form of understanding, and understanding is what makes everything possible.

Compassion gives birth to complicity and, through complicity, in our chest, our mind and our conscience, we are able to receive others into our lives. This gives way to understanding. I needed time to adapt to these new philosophical conclusions.

One day, I realised that I understood everyone and everything. I extended this comprehensive compassion so much that I was able to see everything, myself included, like puppets in the hands of God. I didn't understand that, if we extend this compassion and understanding so far, this feeling is decanted and turns into shame, in a single, black cloud.

"What underdogs we are; we're God's puppets!"

Now, I know that this experience was as a result of my normal side not yet being, at that point, fully accustomed to the other side of me.

I returned from my astral journeys. I would wake up in the morning and there would always be someone waiting there, to listen to my story:

"Why don't I remember like you do? I feel discriminated. I have done everything I can to try and remember things. Why can't I?"

I was surrounded by the energy from these complaints and began to feel guilty for remembering. This feeling of being guilty dulled my sensitivity.

I forgot about my journey. Whilst these people flooded to the churches, to become good parents, adulterating themselves to be able to conquer a socially accepted standard, whilst disconnecting themselves from their essence, I fought to not stray from my path. I managed to keep myself on the other side of society. I prioritised my spirituality and invested in this. I didn't have the lucidity to prevent myself from being contaminated by simply saying to them:

"My chakras didn't just start to open five years ago. In reality, all my life has been dedicated to my spirituality. I paid a very high price during my incarnation, so that I didn't reject my paranormal side. I didn't do as you did, choosing the easiest path, dictated by society and applauded by everyone. I followed other paths, so would be able to arrive at a different destination to you."

At this time, I didn't have lucidity and ended up getting involved in complaints and in other people's problems. I started to want my chakras not to open again. I became worn down as I tried to resist the preconcepts of those people around me, and Mercinha began to re-emerge.

The fanatics swore blindly that, if my chakras opened and I was in a dark place, drinking beer and smoking cigars, then that would be the last time they would ever open. It didn't happen as they had told me it would. I went out to the bars, and the like, but when I returned home, I suffered from sickness and diarrhoea. This time the scars took longer to heal. Thankfully, my chakras continued to open. As the months went by, the blame that I felt disappeared.

Doing things over and over again brings us experience. If we learn from experience, we mature. My relationship with the chakras followed this sequence: the phenomenon, the novelty, the inexplicable. These things were better understood every time they opened.

It was also intense and varied. My spirit friend suggested a few meditations and a specific menu. I learnt to reflect, to meditate and assimilate the relationship that our subtle body has with the foods that suppress our material body.

Depending on the food, we will either grow stronger or weaker, to the point that we could even prevent our subtle body from expressing itself.

All the recommendations that my spirit friend had were intended to help me adapt to a new way of life. I went through so many transformations, and would often question if my soul was the same as when I was born.

*"It's time for you to learn about the transmigration of the soul."* my friend told me whilst we were in one of the institutes in the spiritual sphere. We talked as we walked along the banks of the river of the second Astral House.

"What is transmigration of the soul?"

*"The material body is a product of all the vital organs, such as the heart and liver; as well as the secondary ones, like the extremities. A healthy person will have all these working in harmony. The opposite is where you only appear to be healthy. If an organ is missing then daily life becomes difficult, and the other organs are forced to work harder. This overloading causes energies in the organs to go to the deficient organ. Do you understand what I'm saying?"*

"Yes, the healthy organs transfer their energy to the organ that is weak, to compensate for its lack of energy."

*"Let's use this example of material energy moving to another area to understand the process of transmigration. When chakras join with the glandular circuit, they multiply the amount and refine the quality of subtle, and material, energy. There is a synergy in this interaction. The end result is the integration of the soul. Body and soul joined together bring down the barriers between the consciousness and unconsciousness. The continuity of this process allows the soul to transmigrate."*

"So, does my soul begin to transmigrate?"

*"Yes, as long as there are barriers between our consciousness and our unconscious, our soul suffers loss. It becomes divided like a patchwork quilt. The*

*larger part belongs to the unconscious part of us, whilst the smaller part belongs to the conscious part. It's because of this that people struggle to recall when they leave their physical body as they sleep, as well as other experiences when they incarnate and any other subject that the subtle body would need to access."*

"And my soul? Where will it transmigrate to?"

*"Do you know where your soul is?"*

"Good question!...."

*"Your soul relocated from the conscious part of your mind to the higher consciousness, in a dimension that is more subtle."*

"Do everyone's chakras open?"

*"Yes. The majority of headaches that occur for no apparent reason are our chakras opening. Your sensibility has developed over the course of your incarnations and so, for this reason, they are more noticeable, concrete and amplified for you. Do you remember the exercises we used to do when you were younger?"*

"Yes, the exercises 'to stop me from forgetting'. This is what I used to call them."

*"You need to do the exercises that you were taught when you were little, as well as the ones to align your energies, just like you were taught about with Mãe Helena, Pai Damásio and Pai Nidê. You are following your own path."*

Transmigration of the soul... so was that it?!? I woke up thinking about this, unable to get the idea of it out of my head. Once the chakras had opened, the sensations that I experienced were almost palpable, they were so intense. When I say that I was unable to get these thoughts, and ideas, out of my head, there is no metaphor being used.

After my chakras opened, my ability to think 'received' an extra boost. My thought is almost a voice and exerts great influence over me. Thinking is like obeying; it's not abstract. I clearly understand the strength of my thoughts, as they drive me through life and help me learn. I attribute this strength to my ability to make decisions.

I am totally convinced that a weak thought gives way in someone who is easily manipulated. Someone who has strong thoughts will be able to make their own decisions.

Ever since my chakras opened, I have noticed that my senses have changed. My feeling is a living force that is forever awake and alert. I used to only know the job of feeling through emotions. Now, I have learnt how to differentiate between them.

Feeling is a living force. It is genuine and independent. With regards to emotions, the way in which they manifest will change depending on the external influences that are present at the time.

Because my thoughts, and feelings, were constantly in overdrive, my sensory organs developed and became more acute. This development has become highly visible in the way I act.

My memory has also gone through a number of changes. I can clearly remember making journeys to the spiritual planes and other incarnations.

As we are talking about things that I have learnt to differentiate between, I have also learnt the difference between memory and recollections. A memory is when we remember the feeling, which makes our body react to the emotions. It does not bring with it any mental registration. Recollections are memories of the mind.

When the memory of a feeling causes us to recall something, we are hit with a feeling of nostalgia, and we can cry invisible 'tears'. Depending on the memory, these tears could be either of joy or of sadness.

The mobilization of a recollection brings photographic storylines.

The fusion of a feeling and a thought allows memories to interact. This is the way that I recall my journeys to the astral world, as well as how I remember my other incarnations. Recollections bring images and these are the photographic storyline. The living force of the feeling brings memories and instils a certainty in my mental consciousness.

What we learn in terms of both thoughts and feelings will never leave us. If this isn't the case then, as time goes by, we forget and our memories are replaced.

Astrosophy, for example, was something that I began to study, starting with the Phoenicians, the Greeks, followed by the Christians, in different incarnations.

Through transmigration, I understood my close relationship with Philosophy. If anyone out there is looking for some advice, or a suggestion, I'd always recommend they take up Philosophy or Astrosophy.

Either way, I'm not the same Iaô that rose from the Oxum fountain on Pai Nidê's estate. She is still a part of me. She is a fraction of my consciousness, but by no means the full thing.

These were my first winnings when my chakras opened and when my soul transmigrated.

The photos numbered 7 to 9 record the moment when I started to accept, and internalise, a different life.

\* \* \*

Photo 9 records my first experience of when the crown, or pineal chakra (chakra of the pineal gland), opened.

The physical manifestation of this chakra, as it opened, was completely different to the others. There were no blisters or burns. There was a protuberance, a lump that resembled a small egg.

Whenever this chakra increases activity, the 'egg' grows slightly. When it reduces, it returns to normal. This protuberance has never disappeared.

The doctor once noticed it. It caught him completely off guard. He asked me to undergo computerised tomography tests. It was all okay, apart from the change:

"It's bizarre. It's not negatively affecting your health."

The opening of the crown, or pineal, chakra resulted in my thought patterns becoming more structured and my awareness becoming more acute.

My relationship with other people changed, to the point that I felt they were closer, as if we were all relatives. All I had to do was touch them and I would know what they were feeling and if there was something wrong with their health.

I believe that this is the feeling that is the hardest to be explained. Some people have said that, when I touch them, their skin, their body and their emotions are all aware of a strong feeling. During this period, I was already working as a holistic therapist.

Let me make myself clear: 'holistic therapy' is the name of the therapy society needs, to identify with who I am... So what am I, other than a holistic therapist?

I am Halu Gamashi. I was born as Mércia Celeste Dias da Silva. When I started to walk, I was known as Turunga. At school I was known as Mel. I was called Macarrão when I ran away from home. When I lived in São Paulo, Mel resurfaced. I broke off contact with my father and turned into a rebel called Mercinha. When I moved to Pai Nidê's estate, I became Iaô. I still don't know by what name I will go when I die.

So what do I do about what I am?

I give talks, courses, one-to-one meetings and group lectures, on self-knowledge and Astrosophy and also work as a therapist. I also act as supervisor for a number of health professionals.

I also align energy channels, but this is more restricted and isn't done with everyone, just like Pai Nidê taught me.

It's been eight years since I made myself available to work with the corporal consciousness of my patients. I made a point of using some of the teachings from Pai Nidê, from my spiritual mentor, as well as developing some subtle touch techniques for corporal therapy. Together with Maria Aparecida, a homeopath, I studied phytotherapy treatments. We developed a remedy system based on fruit essences, and I use this system when doing the one-to-ones and also in my groups. I taught some therapists to use this system in their day-to-day work. I called this system: *Sinta* Therapy.

I deliberately separated what I am from what I do. I hope, in time, to discover more things to do out of what I am.

At the time I was writing this book, I used to co-ordinate a study group and would give one-to-one attention to some patients.

Some of the patients told me of the 'charge' they got from my touch, and which they felt course through their skin and flood their emotions. Whilst they reported pleasing sensations, I decided to reduce the number of corporal touch sessions I conducted, and referred these patients on to other therapists, to whom I had passed on my knowledge. So why did I do this?

It was very clear that my chakras were interfering and causing them to feel better. The change didn't come from in them. The aim of my work is for people to cause their own energies to align and to feel a constant well-being that has been generated by their own energy flow.

When my pineal chakra opened, it made me feel whole, free from dichotomy and totally at one with the activity that I was developing. This feeling of being at one greatly improved the quality of the classes I gave: my logic, my oratory and, mainly, my personal magnetism.

I feel that my energy attracts people to me. Many people have already confirmed that I give off this 'vibe' that attracts them. I have to admit that this magnetism has both confused and held me back at times. That said, as the years went by, I came to realise that this magnetism is a concentration of many subtle forces. These forces are the ones that cause people to be attracted. I am the exception to this, in the sense that people are not attracted to me, but to this magnetism, and the subtle energies that flow through me.

I have learnt to differentiate between magnetism and seduction. Seduction results from confusing, and invasive, forces. You can't tell who is suffering from it. Who is the seducer? Who is the person being seduced? Magnetism is the discovery of subtle forces that combine, and manifest, through people.

When I attract someone, I know that the person in question has a similar essence to me and that, together, we are going to do something worthwhile.

The magnetic force to which I refer, in addition to attracting people, also magnetises the collective unconscious, mass particles and etheric volumes that travel round the Earth at the speed of sound. These particles, and volumes, are rich in information, knowledge and wisdom. We call these particles the Akashic Records.

The unconscious is a field of memory that mental consciousness cannot reach. Individual unconscious is personal. Collective unconsciousness is the collection of occurrences that have fallen into the abyss of lost memories, thus creating this field of memory.

Pineal magnetism has the capacity to attach memory to these occurrences and reintegrates it into the collective consciousness, so that it can be incorporated into society.

The Akashic Records are filled with information that, despite having fallen into the abyss of lost memories, never ceased to exist.

Reflecting on the explanation of my friend, with regard to the opening of my crown, or pineal, chakra has led me to imagine the collective consciousness to be like a huge library that goes round the planet. In reality, this is how it happens.

As photos 8 and 9 show, I needed to remove the hair from the area where this chakra is found.

*"Hair is condensed physical energy. You will be freed from pain if you allow the crown chakra to be free from hair."* my spirit friend recommended.

It wasn't an easy period, not by any stretch. Everyone wanted to know why I had shaved my head. They wanted quick responses and brief explanations.

What was I supposed to say? The more people asked me to give them short explanations, the more I realised I wasn't ready and didn't want to talk about it. At the same time, it was also obvious that they weren't open to listening to what I had to say. They didn't want to understand, or assimilate, the complexity of what I was going through.

"This story needs to be written down. You are a phenomenon! Let's find someone who wants to write it for you."

I didn't want this to happen. I was afraid that my experience would be turned into some form of cheap sensation.

In this period, I was living in São Paulo. The number of people that wanted to meet me increased, as did my workload.

The more I help people, and give courses, the more my *raison d'être* is made apparent to the world. I like my work and am satisfied with it.

My chakras didn't stop opening and the capture of Akashic particles increased, and deepened, the transmigration process through which my soul was going. This is a very interesting topic: emigration, transmutation and transmigration. If you are interested in knowing more, I would be more than happy to share my knowledge of this with you. My intention is not to transform this book into an academic discussion.

# End of the 90's

At the end of the 90's, almost ten years had passed since the first time my chakras opened. For the first five years, I was so wrapped up with what was happening to me, I made a point of not allowing outside influences to interfere with my work.

In the latter five years, I wrote a couple of books, I hosted study groups and I threw myself into my work wholeheartedly. Whilst the first half had been filled with fights and conflict when I was looking to be accepted by the group, the second consisted of an internal battle resulting from my experiences and discoveries.

As the solar plexus and root chakras opened, I learnt about the shadowy, dark, dense and agonizing sphere of the collective unconscious. It was the opposite of the Astral Houses and my spirit friends. I have to say that, when these chakras opened, I lost my innocence. I became aware of the existence of adversity, something about which I write in my book: *The Inverted Plane*, edited by Ventos Antigos.

"What is good and evil? The response that is given to this question will differ from person to person…"

This phrase is repeated regularly. Who hasn't said it at some point in their life? That said, I have a deep knowledge of the teachings in this phrase.

The spiritual world also has more than one reality; the philosophical thinking based on the spiritual houses free will and the manipulating attitude of the inverted plane.

Knowing a spiritual current that works to bring people closer to fantastical myths, to slow down human evolution to the point that it runs the risk of driving itself to extinction, is the reason I had an internal battle on such an epic scale. It was a battle that led to disheartenment and showed me that, in order to grow, a huge amount of work is needed; not just work, but also more maturity and lucidity than I ever imagined.

As I have already written two books about the way in which these chakras opened, I won't go into more detail here.

Let's go back to talking about the new chakras that opened in this other phase of my life.

My solar plexus chakra opened in my upper abdomen in the latter part of the '90's and, even to the time of writing this book in February 2004, it has not opened again.

The truth is, during this one opening, I experienced what felt like many openings. It started with a small boil just above my navel. Over the course of the next week, a new boil appeared each day until I had a vertical line made up of seven boils. Like with the other chakras, there was an intense burning when they appeared.

When my solar plexus chakra opened, I felt so afraid. I ended up having so many nightmares, the central focus of which revolved around panic and anguish. I eventually realised that all this fear could not possibly be coming from just me. I investigated and spoke to the people around me at the time. Low and behold, besides my fears, what I was feeling was actually their fear, which had transferred into me. I had suspected this, because I was feeling fears which I had never felt before, which weren't, in fact, mine, such as fear of being alone, travelling at night or being trapped in a lift.

My spirit friend had already spoken to me about the solar plexus chakra and the way in which it is almost like an energy shield that protects, and strengthens, us enabling us to overcome difficulties and have new experiences.

From this, it is likely that this region of the abdomen has dense, negative energies that can be associated with fear, withdrawals and weaknesses.

After this chakra opened, I learnt this lesson with my own body. During an appointment, a patient sat in front of me and I felt tingling in my abdomen, well, my solar plexus area. Suddenly, I started to feel the fears, and feelings, of the patient I was with. When this happened, I temporarily put an end to the consultations. I remembered about an herbal mix I had learnt from Pai Nidê. I made the mix and spread it around where my solar plexus chakra had opened. This made it possible for me to start seeing patients again.

After this, I absorbed information about the fear the patient was feeling, but it was limited to just information rather than the actual fear itself. It didn't stop me from experiencing the peace, and tranquillity, that was needed to be able to help the patient to become stronger and overcome their issues.

Ever since my chakras opened, I have learnt that their main function revolves around the capture, and release, of energy. This first lesson was learnt from the solar plexus chakra, which was invaded by so many types of energy currents. As you may have gathered, this was also a difficult period. I matured during this period and the discomforts disappeared.

A few months later, I experienced my root chakra open for the first time.

Kundalini is an energy. Kundalini is a key. There is a lot that can be said about this energy and key. One of my future aims is to write a book about each chakra. There is so much information to talk about. I don't know if you, the reader, has understood my attempt to synthesize the whole story. Really, to be able to talk about the root chakra, it is first necessary to increase this synthesis.

I will start off by saying that the kundalini is an energy that circulates around our planet. This is the collective kundalini. Individual kundalini circulates between the knee and the genitals. By passing through the genitals, it connects with the sacral chakra. From there, it stops circulating and moves up through the body, all the way to the crown chakra.

The sacral chakra runs from the coccyx to the perineum. Its role is to stimulate, and encourage, development from our base, so that we are able to carry out those activities that are essential to our development. There are basic necessities for us all. There are then choices that are essential for some people to make, whilst those same choices will not have as much of an impact on others. The sacral chakra encourages individualisation and recognition of personal needs.

By understanding the sacral chakra, we are able to understand the root chakra, the role of which is directly related to sexuality. Let's look at two concepts:

•**Sexual activity:** understood to mean a sexual action associated with attraction, appeal or libido.

•**Sexuality:** understood to mean self-esteem, selection, quality, sensuality, sexual love, dance, singing and art in general.

Sexual activity is common in all living things on this planet, as it leads to procreation. Everything in this world that is capable of procreating has sexual energy.

Sexuality is a human addition to this. Man is the only living thing on this planet that is able to use free will with regards to sexuality.

Whilst sexual activity is governed by the root chakra, sexuality is governed by the sacral chakra.

The coccyx is a part of the body that has a selective consciousness, which is used to develop sexuality in humans, so that sexual activity is a more conscious, and selective, act.

This is the path that the kundalini needs to follow, so that man is able to achieve harmony and self-awareness and develop sexual, emotional, intellectual and spiritual evolution.

If this is not the case man is driven, and controlled, by the unbalanced nature of his sexuality and sexual activities (re-read the above definitions I have already provided).

In order to establish an earthly sphere, all energy has two polarities - one negative and the other positive: light and dark, wet and dry, hot and cold. Even in maths, there are positives and negatives:
$$\ldots -5, -4, -3, -2, -1, 0, 1, 2, 3, 4, 5 \ldots$$

It is important to highlight that the concept of positive and negative, in this context, does not refer to good, or bad, qualities. In this world, for energies to work, they need the two polarities: positive (masculine) and negative (feminine).

It's no different with the Kundalini. The Kundalini is the positive polarity for the telluric energy of planet Earth and the telluric energy in man.

Kundala is the negative polarity of this energy, as much for the planet as for man.

The Kundalini is telluric. Telluric is another word for create, generate, allow, make possible, be viable, construct, free, open, give life to, grow, be fruitful, make fertile, shine, develop, manifest, express, etc.

Kundala is anti-telluric. Anti-telluric is another word for to empty.

Please don't confuse the concept of emptying with empty space or nothingness.

Let's think about it for a second; to empty a freezer, it needs to be full. This is emptying something. You find it full and consume everything in it. Emptiness is the space after it has been emptied. Nothingness never had a construction; therefore, it is nothing.

Kundalini energies are intended to fill the planet with life. Before Kundalini energies existed, there was only nothingness. Kundalini energy was the Divine breath that gave life to our planet. All life that exists, exists as a result of this breath.

The four elements are the first, and foremost, manifestations of Kundalini energy. From them came the rivers, the oceans, the fish, the stars and man, etc.

All living things have a Kundalini energy, and this manifests itself in the form of sexual activity. Man is the only living being that has the possibility to change its root energy.

Kundalini energies in man start by circulating between the knees and the genitals. From there, it is attracted to the sacral chakra, which encourages the energy to move up the spinal column. During this process it activates, and unblocks, the path for the pineal chakra (pineal gland).

This preparation is what makes it possible for man to become aware of what is hidden in his unconscious. The way is open for the pineal chakra to be able to access all the hidden information and bring it to the human consciousness. In exactly the same way as it made its way up, the brain fires information down the spinal column.

This is all very complex but, to be able to give an idea of what

I went through when my root chakra opened, I needed to describe the energy and the way in which it works.

The kundala is intended to empty the chakras and the body of manifestations, thoughts, emotions that do not interest us and which unbalance us; for example: hurts, rage, obsessive thoughts, the residue of an inharmonious sexual encounter, etc.

If, at any point, there is a form of unbalance in kundalini or kundala polarity, the effects don't bear thinking about.

A destructive person, someone who spouts nasty remarks, that 'reduce' the astral energy around other people, is an example of what an inharmonious kundala can do. Instead of eliminating and emptying what needs to be eliminated and emptied, it destroys the positive energy, the beauty, the libido and the happiness, etc. It's friction, an internal war, between the kundala and the kundalini energies.

This is the same way that an unbalanced kundala can cause destruction, Armageddon or an apocalypse. One day, we will come back to talking about kundalini energies and the kundala.

When I had access to this information I understood, from my own pineal consciousness, the work that I had done to align my energies with Helena, Damásio and Nidê. I understood, with the same consciousness, the conversations that I had had, and continue to have, with my spirit friend about nothingness, emptiness and transmigration, etc.

When my root chakra opened, it took me on a great 'journey' through the universe. I passed through beauty and ugliness, divinity and hell, the weird and wonderful, purity and tyranny, all of which dwelled within the parallel world existing between kundalini energy and the kundala.

Kundalini sexual energy showed me sexual love; a harmonic exchange of pleasure. I survived and continue to live with an orgasm of the soul. I survived because it is a powerful experience; to allow yourself to be ravished by an orgasm of the soul. The energy discharge is intense. It is a kind of spiritual enlightening.

It is an experience that leads to the death sphere. It takes you and you go. I have felt death. It is like extinguishing a light, losing love, feeling pain. During this moment, it was like I was both mother and father to everything, my own body included.

I got out of bed, opened the window and looked out at the world, which I now saw for the first time. It was in me. After these experiences, everything had changed. My ability to love had grown. I love more and better, and this goes for loving myself, my friends, the elements, life and nature. I have to admit that this feeling is something quite special.

When my root chakra opened, I also felt the kundala's sexual energy; there is no end to it, and it feels as if the best is yet to come.

As you wait, you become excited, believing that 'it will happen', but that joyful release never comes. What comes is a spasm, an orgasm deriving from exhaustion, a tremor, an emotional crisis and a troubled mind. Afterwards, there's emptiness and a feeling of only hunger or thirst. In the attempt to feel something more profound you do it again and, again, you experience exactly the same thing.

These types of experience cause our egos to become fragile and drive us to find escape routes using alcohol, drugs, overindulgence, etc… This is how man becomes egocentric, thinking only of himself. The capacity to love dissipates and you go through life from there, dragging your body, feeling unloved and finding it difficult to love, and care for, other people.

If the collective, and individual, kundalini energies don't align, the human race cannot survive. How could it? With man increasing his egocentrism, those who are most powerful reach the top. From there, the wars start: cold, religious, competitive, etc.

The experience of capturing these thoughts and questions in my own body brought a lot of movement into my life. The movement of fear, for instance, caused me to stop talking, made me run away, made me believe that I was mad.

"This is madness! I'm sick; it's the only explanation." I used to repeat to myself.

"The fear is making you think like that. If you let the fear win, your entire life will have been in vain." the mute voice, that forever accompanied me, used to tell me.

Defeated by the fear, cowardice seeped in. I wanted the whole world to believe me; for us to join together and take a stand.

"If no-one wants to listen to me, if no-one believes me… I

tried, I did my part. The others didn't do theirs."

The cowardice passed and I began to reflect. I cried so much. I decided to undergo another energetic experience with the four elements, to understand what I would really do with my story, my *raison d'être*. I returned to Bahia.

I looked for someone that I once knew, given that Nidê was no longer around, and with his guidance, I renewed the strength of the four elements. I needed such strength, and courage, to be able to believe in myself and push forward with what I knew I was supposed to do.

Some people who were around me left. They thought I had changed. These people only preferred to be around Halu Gamashi when she was experiencing fear and cowardice.

During the time I'm talking about, I used to wait for the influential people I used to work with to help me with my *raison d'être*. There were so many meetings, so many conversations, projects, endless dinners and never-ending trips. They could never know enough 'important people'.

"Halu, we need to involve some Tom, Dick and Harry. The one that you indicated isn't influential. How could he help?"

I lived through the battle, whilst carrying on down my own path, with less influential people and, it's because of this, that I have been able to understand what I needed to do in order to actually accomplish something.

The people who remained in the group spent the next two years aligning their energies.

Then the persecution started. People I loved dearly, yet who did not understand, turned against me.

"I know that your work with energy is not the same as this desecrated and commercialised Candomblé. I know that your relationship with the elements in nature is completely different to the unmeasured and dogmatic slaughter you hear talked about. But, if you continue to talk about aligning energy, people are going to become confused. They're going to distance themselves from you and they're going to leave."

There was no point me saying this, but people needed to know, and understand, the true language about aligning energy. This is an ancient, safe tool that was used to help man achieve under-standing and enlightenment.

There was no point me saying that the work needed to align energy was only the beginning, even though the main aim remained unchanged. Through this work, people would have the strength to learn how to handle the light, etc.

I realised that I needed to move on, or else run the risk of ev-erything careering off course in the form of a discussion that leads nowhere. A change in approach was needed.

I left for Bahia, armed with the 'prophecy' that was now weighing heavy on my shoulders: the people in the study groups were going to leave because I was putting forward ideas that were exotic or primitive. When I returned, I invested in people, talked to them and many came back and now remain by my side. The major-ity didn't leave. They liked the type of work we were doing and brought in their siblings, mothers, fathers, friends, all of whom wanted to know about Halu Gamashi's new proposal.

The 'prophecy' didn't come to pass. It didn't come to pass, despite me having made clear that my work was not the mirror im-age of traditional Candomblé, despite me having made clear that en-ergy alignment is a type of work that involves the four elements and food and dance. Some people stayed, whilst others left.

I accepted this; people need to do what they believe right. There will always be people who want to destroy those of us that work to build.

Inharmonious kundalini and kundala energies cause people to turn into 'soldiers'. They don't respect free will and think they can, and should, destroy any idea that they disagree with.

I survived the inquisition. My work continues on towards the light, as well as on towards my spirit friends, towards the Orishas, towards my colleagues, to my country which still allows freedom of expression.

This unusual war served as an example for me to understand how important it is to be strong and balanced, to be able to manage the energy of other people.

During this period, I also experienced the chakras in the cen-tre of my feet (lower synesthetic chakras) open. I didn't get a photo of this. I'm still not fully aware of what happened when these chakras opened. I knew I was stronger, more determined and started to better manage my faults, in the sense that I was able to identify and work on improving them.

I believe this outcome is the result of each of the chakras having opened and the work that I have done and continue to do. I still don't believe that I am in a position to be able to describe what happened when the lower synesthetic chakras opened.

I was told by a friend that, to be able to describe something, you must first have a good understanding of it. Let's see if I have any further experiences with these chakras opening. If I do, then I will be able to better share with you what happened and what I have gone through.

I am, however, able to say that I noticed that my body, and mind, now feel more rooted and purposeful. What my head wants is for my feet to have the strength to go in search of something more concrete.

The upper and lower synesthetic chakras are connected to laterality, spatial awareness and the harmony of the ethereal being. Unbalance in the orbits of these chakras brings uncertainty and lack of strength. It results in the auric field becoming more dense and leads to depression and anxiety.

As you can see in photos 4 and 13, when my upper synesthetic chakras opened in the centre of my hands, this helped to eliminate any unbalance I had.

This is what it is; I learnt everything though my body. As a writer, I am aware that a book can inspire us, stimulate us and inform us. Just don't allow yourselves to be fooled, my friends; a book, or theory lesson, will not be sufficient to teach us anything. A book can tell us a story, but it's not powerful enough to turn us into a living character in that same story.

Would you like a suggestion?

Get involved in the things you have an interest in studying. Get right in there; have fun, do as I did with Pai Nidê. Don't give up!

People who want life to save them are prepared to die for it! Be the person who keeps life safe within yourself and encourage those around you to do the same and save their own lives.

The wise are those who have wisdom, but who has that?

Someone who lives life whilst knowing the price that must be paid for doing so.

Pay attention to what the wise ones say. Are they happy? No. They're 'special'. We should want to be like rice; be the same, no matter where we are or at which table we are served. When there is no rice, you know something is lacking, as it can be an accompaniment to any other dish. These people, these 'rice people' are aware of the entire world without ever losing contact with others like them.

I am Halu Gamashi, one of the 'rice people'. I have never, nor will ever, allow the unusual part of me to stop me from being at every table, in every body, everywhere where I'm needed.

I was part way through my journey when I started to write this book; somewhere between courage and fear. At the end of my journey, I have managed to develop the courage to tell you; don't let yourself be influenced by my story! Go, live your own adventure! If I were able to help you, I would. I love adventures.

It's clear that I still have a great deal left to say. Be patient, both with me and with yourself.

Out of everything that I have left to say, one thing remains the same and that's my initial statement; I am a normal person with a not so common gift, striving to unite two worlds and merge them into one.

My God is the God of eternal love and strength!

My religion is the world and all the people in it; my religion is nature. I am reconnected with everything that is good for me, with everything that owns me and with everything that is owned by me.

With love,

*Halu Gamashi.*

Summer, February 24, 2004
Santana do Parnaíba, São Paulo, Brazil

# Appendices

Reflections on my story

# 1. What is birth?

One day, a son approached his father, saying he had dreamt that he had learnt to cut wood:

"In my dream, I grabbed an axe, cut down the tree and drank the sap. As I drank the sap, I understood what it was to be a tree. I hit the tree I'd cut down and knew that it was wood. I then made tools out of the wood."

The boy's father listened in silence, taking in what the boy was saying before speaking:

"You need to fulfil this dream. I'll send you to a place where there are many trees you can cut down and turn into wood."

The boy set out on the journey having been given ninety years, by his father, in which to realise the dream. Ninety years can seem like a lifetime for some, yet the blink of an eye for others. That said, in all honesty, ninety years isn't that long, nor is it a short period of time. Ninety years is the time given by the father to the son to fulfil the dream.

The boy's father could now turn time into something that he would be able to count. To do this, the father created life, made spaces and created Heaven and Earth.

Life + Spaces + Planets and stars = time that can be counted.
Time that can be counted – life = wasted time.
Time that can be counted – space = hard times.
Time that can be counted – Planets and stars = time that is blind, deaf and mute.

The father created, for the son, life. It generated trees in space. He inseminated the stars to feed his son in distant spheres. Space with trees that could be cut down and turned into wood. By doing this, the boy would make the most of his life in order to realise his dream.

The boy left. He found the trees; he slept in their shade and he feasted on their fruit. He went back to sleep; woke up again; ate, slept, woke up, ate...

Ninety years passed by and the boy's father called him back.

When he saw his father, the son remembered the reason he had set out on his journey to far off lands:

"Father, I was distracted by the shade and the fruit from the trees. They were so good. I got sleepy and, every time I grew sleepy, I forgot all about the dream I had. Give me another opportunity."

The boy's father listened in silence, then did as his son asked. He offered him another eighty years. He created life, space and created Heaven and Earth so that his son would be able to fulfil his dream. To those people out there that think eighty years are less than ninety, I say:

"It's not more, nor is it less. In this story, eighty years is simply the period of time given to the son, by his father, in which to realise the dream."

The boy set out on a second journey. He found the trees, went back to sleep in the shade and went back to feasting on the fruit. He went back to sleep, he devoured fruit, slept in the shade. The more he slept, the more he wanted to sleep and the more he forgot, the more he drifted off...

The eighty years that his father gave him passed by. At the end of this time, when the boy saw his father again, he remembered the trees, the wood, his dream and everything else.

"Father, what is it about the trees that makes me forget about the reason for my journey?"

His father answered: "The trees possess their own life and they know that you want it for yourself. The trees are wise. Why would they give this knowledge up to someone who isn't working for it? You did the complete opposite. You allowed yourself to be seduced by them. You proved you were unable to turn them into wood, so they turned you into someone who didn't pose a threat."

"Trees only give their wisdom to those who deserve it. The trees know that, once they are in the hands of a wise man, they will be reborn."

"Give me another chance, Father!"

The boy's father listened in silence, before giving in to the request. He counted out, and offered his son, another seventy years in which to realise his dream. Now, for those who believe that each chance the father gives to his son reduces his time, allow me to clarify:

"Seventy years is no more or less than eighty years; seventy years is the duration of the third opportunity the father gave his son to fulfil his dream."

The boy set out. Before eating the fruit from the trees, he started work. As he worked, he grew tired. As he grew tired, he became hungry and sleepy. Despite being very tired, the boy did not eat as he had done before. He ate less because he also needed to sleep. He slept and dreamt of the axe he would use to cut down the trees and extract the sap he would then drink, in order to become wise like the tree. He woke up. He remembered, and did as he had done in the dream, returning afterwards to his father, his dream fulfilled.

"Father, I did it! I did it!"

"In the first, and second, attempts you ate three times the amount you needed to and left in your wake the seeds from those fruits that you wasted."

He was, of course, referring to the seeds inside the fruits when he said this.

"Your being there caused a domino effect, one that only you would be able to end. The seeds you left behind grew into trees which, in turn, created the shade for you to sleep in. When you only ate what was necessary, the seeds grew into the trees that replaced the ones you had cut down to create wood. Whilst you were eating the fruit and not cutting down the trees, the leftover seeds grew. They increased the amount of shade that was there and reduced the amount of natural light available to you. It's not wise to upset the natural balance of nature and, where possible, we should avoid doing this at all costs. You will return and cut down the trees that your greed created."

And so what his father foresaw came to pass and the balance was restored.

**Moral of the story:**

Living is learning how not to upset the natural balance. If we upset it, we disturb the natural flow of time that is given to us – just as the boy did with the time given to him by his father. Time can appear to pass faster, or slower, depending on the way in which the balance is upset. For this reason, we should only do what is necessary and then make sure that we use the energy flowing through our bodies. As a result, everything we do or eat, if we use the example from the story, returns back to the Earth and is reborn. If the energies aren't reborn, then we'll never move forward, at least not until we have learnt the lesson we are supposed to learn.

# 2. What is death?

There was once a tailor who lived in a village. He spent his life tailoring clothes to fit each, and every, villager who came see him. He knew everything there was to know about clothe sizes and the needs of those for whom he worked. Once he had altered the size of a garment, he would call the respective villager and would exchange old clothes for the new ones. The old, and worn out, clothes that were brought to him were given a new lease of life, reborn all fresh as if new.

He was such a skilled tailor. Everything he touched was made new, regardless of how many times the garment had been worn out and brought back to him. Life was good, until one day there was an uprising in the village:

"Let us be the ones to decide what our clothes look like! We don't always like what you design! Look at my trousers. They're so short. I've grown and you haven't altered them. I'm the butt of all my friends' jokes."

"So, you think that your trousers are short because you've grown?"

"Exactly! I want longer trousers, ones that cover my legs down to my feet, just like my parents and friends."

The tailor listened to the villager's complaints and went home. The next day, when he returned, the complaints and abuse started again:

"I want another pair of trousers; these ones are no good to me. Why don't you listen to me? It's not fair that you offer me the short trousers and longer ones to everyone else. My feet are bare to the world. I want another pair of trousers. Everyone laughs at me because they can see my feet."

The tailor tried in vain to convince the villager this was not true and went as far as suggesting that many may, in fact, have thought it a better look. To avoid causing problems for himself, or any more of an uprising in the village, the tailor agreed to make the alterations for the villager if, for no other reason, than to teach the villager a lesson. The tailor took the villager to where he worked, where he then made the alterations. The villager was beyond happy with his new trousers, which now reached down to the floor. However, when he tried to walk, he tripped over them and fell to the floor. He wasn't used to walking with such long trousers. He would stand, take a step, then fall; stand, take a step, then fall. This continued all day.

"Tailor, I can't walk!"

"I know and knew this when I made the alteration for you!"

"So, what do I do now? Make them shorter!"

"I'm not just here for your convenience. If you think longer trousers would be better for you, and they weren't, what makes you think that shorter ones will be any different? Besides, I have other people that need my assistance. I'll turn up the bottom of the trousers for you, back to the length they were."

"No! I want the originals back; they were better!"

"I had to ruin the first pair to make you the second, as *you* requested."

He turned up the trousers for the villager as he said this, before going on to say:

"You'll have these! If you do come back to me asking for them to be made longer, it'll just be a simple case of turning them down again."

"Will I have to have these for good?"

"You'll have these until you learn to walk in trousers that reach down to the floor. So, I'll call you and we'll see how you're getting on at the time. Now, go."

The villager left with his newly turned down trousers, waiting to grow.

This is what it is to die. Dying is exchanging clothes. When the tailor calls for us, we exchange our vest and body for one that is more suitable for the next life. If we decide to go to the tailor, to complain about the incarnation we have, or with the task or the life that we have, we are asking the tailor to provide us with a garment that is in keeping with our own delusion. We stop walking and growing. We double the problems that we have, just like the villager in the story.

# 3. Questions and answers

"What is a lie?"

"Lies are the truth that God told and then hid from the messenger. As he believes that he is telling a lie, his truth is hidden."

"What is truth?"

"Truth is a discovery. Everything we discover turns out to be the truth."

"What are discoveries?"

"Discoveries are personal conclusions."

"What are conclusions?"

"A conclusion is where a journey ends. Only someone who has reached the end of their journey knows what a conclusion is."

"What is the end of a journey?"

"Go and live life to the full, one experience at a time. Then you will know what the end of a journey is."

"What does 'live life to the full' mean?"

"Live life to the full means show yourself to the world. Only someone who shows him or herself to the world truly lives life to the full. If you hide away from the world, you will lose yourself and think that real life is a lie."

# Letters

# 1. For the teachers out there

*"To educate is not to persuade..."*

Persuasion is a conclusion; we look at the world and, through this look, we imprint on our body and soul the information we see, all of which comes from different sources: family, schools, books, the media, etc. At any given moment, these energies converge to a single point that takes us over. This is persuasion.

When a single source of information wants to do everything alone, we experience frustration. If the mistake is then admitted, if we experience a sense of humility, we change our trajectory and understand that dictatorships don't allow us to grow. If this doesn't happen, after frustration comes rebellion and humiliation and it's this that goes forward.

Education is, above all, the ability to understand that nobody is powerful enough, on their own, to be able to transmit the information to whoever they want.

As a consequence of this reflection, I think back to children and to teenagers and can't forget the thing that most characterises them; their openness to stimuli. Children and teenagers experience this responsibility at its most extreme. They allow themselves to be stimulated by these intellectual, and emotional, sources that stem from a simple childish curiosity.

When we become adults, we tire of this. I also can't forget the feeling of happiness and satisfaction that we, as adults, feel if we were allowed to enjoy these stimuli as youngsters.

Education is at the base of all the stimuli and cannot abandon this post. Chaos exists when education stops being the base and we race straight to the point of arrival rather than focus on the point we started out from; this is the function of persuasion.

We need to give our children, and teenagers, a solid base and this is only possible with 'friend education', free from the weight of persuasion. Oh yes, this is important. Children and teenagers are highly stimulated by this stage of life and will have the attributes that will enable them to persuade, to develop and be educated. They will value these attributes and, when it is their turn to educate, they will carry with them the intrinsic friendship that a teacher should have.

With love to all teachers,
*Halu Gamashi*

# 2. For all those people who have faith, belief and wisdom

Faith is an intention to believe. Belief is the basic deepening of knowledge that gives us wisdom. The main difference is the posture and the behaviour of each. We use faith as a means to request help in a situation that we feel is difficult.

"Faith can move mountains." This is what Christ said. Faith can help us in every situation. It makes us strong and teaches us to believe. With belief, we are able to do what needs to be done; solve problems, to the extent that those people around us, who do not yet believe in themselves, are able to develop faith by understanding our beliefs.

Wisdom is what follows from belief. By deepening our knowledge, we are able to understand the polarities to all questions. You don't have to be a problem solver to know, and understand, how to avoid problems to begin with.

Anyone who has not known peace, but who has heard people talk about it, has faith that one day we will achieve it. They take part in its realisation and, when we achieve it, they wholeheartedly believe in its existence. They let it seep into their lives and they coexist with it. They believe that, when it leaves, to be able to reclaim it would entail developing techniques to keep it and, from there, they develop wisdom.

An ardent is someone who asks for help. Someone who is credulous helps themselves. A wise man is someone who completes the tasks that are necessary in the transformation process.

The risk that someone who is ardent runs is accommodation. The ardent abuses his faith, as it is always there to help and guide him and, therefore, he is unable to move forward and become credulous.

The ardent hasn't learnt anything from all the lessons about faith. Every difficulty he encounters always makes him go running back to his faith and makes him disregard the previous lesson.

Someone who is credulous runs the risk of repeating themselves. They believe that they are self-sufficient and so the quantum leap, in search of wisdom, is not sufficient. They are passive when difficulties start and wait for the problems to reach their peak, so that they may act as a provider.

The risk of wisdom is isolation. The balance consists of being alert to the changes in time. With every new message that is given you go looking for faith, so that you can reflect it, implement it, until the moment that it is confirmed as being real and true. As a result you divulge it, knowingly, to inspire faith in other people.

I have faith in God and believe that he will help me through the hard times.

I believe in God. For this reason, I abide by his Commandments and take responsibility for my actions.

I know God. I understand that life alternates between us winning and losing; that we will go through both good times and bad. In the good times I become stronger, in preparation for the times that aren't so good. During the times of light, I enlighten myself so that I am able to make it through the dark times.

I have faith in all those who have developed faith.

I believe in all those who share their experiences, so that they can develop internal beliefs.

With a devotional love for all those who are wise,
*Halu Gamashi*

# 3. For the scientists out there

Doubt doesn't create insecurity.

The above phrase is likely to get you thinking, at first... This was my intention; to make you, as the reader, reflect on the question.

Think about it; if you are unable to control doubt, the only outcome is uncertainty.

When an element of doubt creeps into our lives, the truth is that we are shielding ourselves from another element: surprise. Doubt is an alert that signals the arrival of a task that we need to be prepared for and focused on, in order to be able to achieve importance and depth.

For as long as we are processing doubt, our emotions are able to mature and our intellect prepares to decode what is happening to us.

For these reasons, it's advisable not to be afraid of doubt. By fearing it, we prevent ourselves preparing for it. Instead, it is better to give in to it and allow our minds to investigate and find the reasons for its appearance.

When we are given a task we do on a daily basis, we don't experience doubt. We don't need it because we are already ready for such tasks.

Doubt indicates the arrival of something new. Cast it aside and allow the surprise to take you. Guided by the element of surprise, we throw ourselves into the unknown, the positive outcome of which does not depend on our direction. As a result, we experience childish feelings of achievement. On the other hand, negative outcomes also do not depend on our direction; we point the finger and blame others; we experience childish pain.

Doubt gives way to different outcomes. We become alchemists in our own lives. If the outcome is negative, we are able to see where we went wrong; we experience an apprentice's disappointment. If the outcome is positive, we revel in what we have done, taking what we have learnt from the experience and carrying it with us throughout the rest of our lives.

We should aim to treat doubt with the respect it deserves, so that it will continue to visit us and help us further mature.

Love to all those who allow themselves to feel doubt, as they believe that doubt can recycle beliefs.

*Halu Gamashi*

# 4. For all those born after 1940

We run the risk of turning into that which once scared or humiliated us.

We are born with a responsibility to strive to improve our collective conscience.

Our task is to explore, and scrutinise, tradition and to have the authority to discover new values, to question paradigms and set our thoughts free from the fragile, and limited, basis of materialism.

We run the risk of doing the opposite and transforming ourselves into mirror images of conscious tyranny.

In order to turn order on its head, it is necessary to be completely detached from the polarity that we don't want any more.

We need to awaken in the Age of Aquarius. It's an age that will strengthen our fraternity, group life and originality, each of which is a tool that enables us to be conscious living things whilst, at the same time, bringing down the barriers and borders of the collective unconsciousness.

When we talk about the collective and say we want to live in a group, it becomes necessary to go through with it and to share our experiences.

In my opinion, we run the risk of being shipwrecked in our work by being so attached to the traditional values, such as those relating to money, fame and power.

It is very common, even if we don't achieve one or more of these aims, for artists, politicians and thinkers who proclaim peace, fraternity and all the other items that the Age of Aquarius brings with it.

However, we don't know how to manage fame, money, success and power. These laws belong to the past. We were built on aquarium mortar, which acts as the foundation for the values held by the people of planet Earth. We maintain the intention of this mortar and there are people who turn into leaders of 'Peace and Love', 'Green thumbs' and 'Save Freedoms'!

Movement after movement was initiated to make man wake up to the reborn, true values. However some, perhaps the majority, were not able to give up the excess comfort and security that fame, success and money can bring.

We 'embark' into the Renaissance. On achieving fame, we became the same as our parents. We need to invert this framework so that we can achieve our own goals.

We live in a confusing time, where people who look to God instigate war. People who sing about love, create competition. We elect leaders that betray nations. Art is mixed with alienation.

Contemporary brothers, our work has increased. We need to go back to the start. We wash from our faces those traits that make us similar to our tyrants.

With love for us all,
*Halu Gamashi*

# About The Author

Halu Gamashi was born in the Northeast of Brazil, Bahia. Therapist for more than 20 years and responsible for creating subtle mind, body and energy techniques. She teaches and completes workshops about aura energy, astrosophy, philosophy, health and human behaviour in various Brazilian and European cities. Due her own ancestral culture journey, Gamashi's books outline the amplification of cosmic consciousness and the spontaneous awakening of the chakras.

* * *

It is interesting to note that, over the course of her life, Halu has gone by different names; some she was given, others she created, yet they all contributed to who she is today. She recognises herself as being not one person, but several, as she wants to rediscover the intra-individual plurality that makes her who she is. She sees herself constantly at one with the world and with the people in it. The varying descriptions, described in this book, do not make her isolate herself in her individuality, nor does it make her retreat into herself. Instead, it takes her to another level of consciousness, that of the subtle body. Her 'Id', which is capable of learning, and living, in different places and under adverse conditions is, therefore, also capable of being guided by the cosmic loom, i.e. the transformation into becoming a cosmic Id so as not to just experience the lineage of living things, and their historical ascendance, but also to open herself up to the universal fatum. Through this, she connects herself to the tree of life in all its forms, from the most basic, to the most Divine.

*Rosa Dias*

Web site: http://www.VentosAntigos.com
Facebook: https://www.facebook.com/VentosAntigos/

Made in the USA
Las Vegas, NV
15 December 2023

82926032R00128